Common Sense Business

Redefining the Way that We Operate

Our Lives and Our Businesses

by

MARK A. ZARR

Common Sense Publishing
www.CommonSenseDevelopment.com

www.markzarr.com

CONTENTS

SEVEN THINGS YOU NEED FOR SUCCESS (OR NOT): HOW TO WEED THROUGH EVERYONE'S OPINIONS

As business owners, we have the distinct privilege of being under constant bombardment from other people's opinions about how we should run our businesses. We are inundated with dozens, if not hundreds, of conflicting thoughts on how business should be run. From peer-reviewed college studies, to journalists, to business consultants, there is never a lack of theory and opinion. So how do we weed through the clutter to find the real gems?

I have studied business from the academic perspective, I have lived business as a business owner and as an employee, and I have gained new insights from business experts willing to share their wisdom. Each opportunity for learning has given me new perspectives, new ways to approach problems, and a greater understanding of the simplicity of business. That's right, I said simplicity. Everything I have witnessed and learned has shown me that there is no complex equation to business. Business success is built on common sense. Common sense that says business is about working hard, thinking straight, and managing with integrity.

As a young college senior, I was interning with Target® in their management training program. I was eager to learn all about the tricks of the trade that made Target tick as a successful retail giant. What I found was a company committed to the basics: fair prices, reliable products, and good customer service. In all honesty, training to be a manager was easy. It was long hours and hard work, but there were no secrets, complicated formulas, or overly cumbersome duties. This first dose of reality hit me hard. I had just spent the last four years

1

studying business from the perspective of the scientific method. College made business sound like rocket science or chemistry. Not three weeks into the real world, I was faced with the contradiction between the study of business and the practice of business. The experience was invaluable. It sent me down a journey that I never expected. The contradiction helped open my eyes to what really mattered in business and it launched my never-ending pursuit to find the truth among all the opinions.

1. Common sense tells us that customers want to be treated fairly and with respect. (Customer Service)

2. Common sense tells us that customers want quality and value in the things they buy. (Research and Development)

3. Common sense tells us that a business should not spend more than it makes. (Accounting)

4. Common sense tells us that if we want more money, we need more customers. (Marketing)

5. Common sense tells us that employees want to be treated fairly and with respect. (Human Resources)

6. Common sense tells us that if we want to be successful, we have to work hard. (Leadership Development)

7. Common sense tells us to act with integrity. (Ethics)

That's right: all that the experts and university professors are doing is finding complicated ways of explaining and defining common sense. Your whole business perspective changes once you realize that the secret to business is that it is not that complicated. Your success depends only on your ability to apply common sense to your daily routine. Don't let the web of opinions and business theories distract you from your goal. You already have all of the important skills that you need to succeed. The technical stuff follows with trial and error.

This book focuses on the seven common sense principles. The goal is to take the complication out of business. The purpose is to come away with a better, simpler explanation of what makes businesses succeed. We are not going to use any complicated terminology or high-level theory. We are going to focus on applicable and implementable techniques, mindsets, and tricks of the trade. The book is focused on solving real world, actual problems that every business faces.

The first step to creating greater success is to work smarter not harder. This age-old adage may seem corny but it speaks the truth. For too long, business has been hijacked by complicated theories and explanations, but let's face it, all we really want is to pay our bills and grow our business. Today, things have been blown out of proportion and this book will help bring business back to bite size.

THE MEDIA EFFECT

We can't complete a study on weeding through opinions without realizing that besides universities and experts, the media also has a large impact on our thoughts about business. Unfortunately, the media only focuses on bad news and finding someone to blame for that bad news. If you only get your business perspective from the media, you will quickly become very depressed. We must learn that the media does not control our economy or our business. Only we, as business owners, are responsible for our success or failure.

The media loves to blame poor economic times on government and global economic failures. Though these are factors, we need to learn to move past these obstacles and get back to the heart of business. Our economy is built off of a relationship, not between government and business, but between the people and business. Our economy is based on the idea that whoever provides the best product and service at a price people are willing to pay wins. This agreement between people and business is what drives us forward. The problem is that we have forgotten this fact. Large corporations don't have to innovate because they can just be bailed out. But that is ok, because small business is still more powerful than the huge corporations. People want good, local, honest organizations and only the small business can provide such things.

You are the driver of your own economy. If it is a down economy, make it turn. Run your business to the best of your ability. Provide quality products and caring services; create innovative new ways of doing business; most importantly, keep your head up. Let the newscasters speculate and let the politicians negotiate because while they are doing that, we will be rolling up our sleeves and doing what we do best.

COMMON SENSE IN PRACTICE

List three areas of your business that you would like to simplify:

1._____ 2._____ 3._____

Do you think there are any preconceived ideas that get in the way of your business? Explain:

_____
_____
_____
_____
_____
_____
_____
_____
_____

Boiling everything about your business down, what are the three things that really make your business tick?

1._____ 2._____ 3._____

Common Sense Notes (Use this section to write about whatever stood out do you about this lesson):

_____
_____
_____
_____
_____
_____
_____
_____
_____
_____

SECRET FORMULA FOR SUCCESS: H.A.P.P.I.N.E.S.S.

Have you ever met an unhappy business owner? Of course you have! Most likely they were not all that successful, right? It may seem like too much common sense to even point out that unsuccessful people aren't happy. However, I would argue that the unhappiness part comes first. Unhappy people aren't successful. Ok, so what I am really talking about is attitude. In order to succeed, you have to first believe in yourself. If you're like me, this may seem like hogwash, but the more I study this idea, the stronger it becomes.

We often make life and our circumstances a lot harder than they have to be. We really only have two options: we can control our emotions or be controlled by them. There is no middle ground. Now, before you go throwing this book out, thinking that is just preaching more self-help, control-the-universe mumbo-jumbo, let me explain. I understand you have heard this kind of stuff before. Think happy thoughts and you can will success toward your direction. You can't help but think, "Great, where's the fairy dust to go along with my happy thoughts?" The truth is that there is nothing magical or mysterious about the fact that your thoughts shape your attitude and your attitude will dictate what you are willing to do. For example, if all you think about are problems and issues, then your attitude will be one of worry and fear. However, if you spend your energy thinking of solutions and ways to move your business forward, then your attitude will be full of energy and excitement.

I don't believe that you can will the universe to bring you success, or even be assured of riches as long as you put out good karma and only think positive thoughts. I do, however, believe that we can, and should, control our attitude and, more importantly, our emotions. People that explode at the drop of a hat or assume that the world is ending every time something unexpected happens can't make effective decisions on a normal day, let alone in times of crises. It is extremely important to learn how to control your emotions, think rationally,

5

and see the forest through the trees. In order to present yourself as a professional, you must be able to understand and control your emotions. In order to manage people, you first have to be able to manage yourself. In order to understand others, you have to first understand yourself.

Those who are self-aware (able to control their emotions) are also very good at self-managing and self-motiving. They also have the ability to judge their own strengths and weaknesses and ask for help. It is very important to be able to recognize your limitations so that you can properly delegate, ask for assistance, and get the right training to improve your business. Those who think they can do everything on their own are normally the first to curl up into a ball and give up when the going gets tough. However, those who can self-manage tend to be very energetic and optimistic, because they understand who they are and what they are working for, and just in case you missed it the first time, they now when to ask for help.

Another way of looking at the power of the proper attitude is to face the fact that people don't like to be around sad, depressed, and whiny individuals. In order to be effective in business, you must be able to present yourself, and your business in a positive light. After all, in the business world, you are constantly selling yourself. The right attitude will help insure that you always represent yourself as a successful and forward thinking individual. Put yourself in the shoes of the client or customer; when you walk into a restaurant or store, you want to be welcomed by smiling, happy, and helpful people. Attitude is everything.

BUILDING THE RELATIONSHIP

Business is all about making connections and building relationships. If you aren't liked by your clients and customers you are not going to sell to them. This may seem obvious, but don't let the simplicity of the idea discount the importance. Going back to the original argument that unhappy people aren't successful, let us examine why happy people are successful. Happy people, or people with positive attitudes, don't let their emotions control their actions. They understand that only they are responsible for their success and they don't blame circumstances or others for their failures. People with positive attitudes look for solutions rather than problems and when they do run into issues, they see them as opportunities for improvements and innovation versus road blocks. The biggest reason that happy people are more successful is because they are likable. No matter what their business is, they build it on a foundation of strong relationships, relationships with their employees, vendors, and customers. This relationship focus helps them create lasting and meaningful partnerships with everyone around them. Most importantly, happy people always are looking for ways to help others. This others-first mentality allows happy people to find new products and services to assist their customers and new ways of connecting with people.

I have found that there are four things that successful (we'll call them happy) people share. These four things are basic, but it is the simplicity that makes them powerful. In a world where sincerity is on the verge of extinction, being honest and down to earth with people can go a long way.

1.   **Happy People Ask Questions That are Relevant and Thought Provoking.** By getting to know what is important to your customers, you will always be looking for ways to improve your products and services to meet the needs of those around you. By truly engaging people, you will approach business from a position of servanthood. Your business should be more about fulfilling a calling than simply turning a profit and your sincerity should always come through. This will help people be more willing to trust and do business with you.

2.   **Happy People Use Humor.** People like to laugh but, more notably, they like to work with people who they can relate to. Humor shows that you are down to earth and relatable, especially if you can make fun of yourself (just don't make fun of the customer or other people). Humor can get tricky because many people think that this means they have to be comedians and they end up forcing humor. The best way to think about using humor is to simply let your guard down. Remember that you are asking your customers to become your friend. In order to do this, you need to be professional but approachable.

3.   **Happy People Give Away Value.** Everyone likes free samples. Your free samples should be a constant preview of how your skills, experience, and knowledge will benefit your clients. Write a blog, send out newsletters, give keynote presentations, submit articles to a local paper or magazine, teach a free business skills class. The key here is that you are selling yourself as an expert. If you try to use any of these mediums to sell your products, it will backfire on you. There is nothing people hate more than showing up for a free seminar and then being forced to just sit through a sales presentation about the benefits of a product, and no one will ever read a blog about why your product is better than all the rest. For example, if you offer health products, a better route would be to write a blog about healthy living and lifestyle choices or offer a free class on preparing healthy foods.

4.   **Happy People Promote Happy Customers.** Everyone knows the power of a testimony, but most people don't really know how to use them correctly. Unfortunately, having a couple of testimonies on your website or offset on your marketing materials will not get you the results that you are looking for. People know the difference between a real review and carefully selected quotes attached to a sales piece. The most effective idea is to promote your clients. If you are sending your clients referrals, they will be more likely to do the same for you.

Business is really all about attitude. If you believe that nothing can make you fail, then you will be willing to do whatever it takes to succeed. The wrong attitude will tear down relationships, but a positive attitude will always bring you more opportunities. Happiness may not be the only factor in creating long lasting success, but it will certainly go a long way in helping. When people can trust and depend on you, it is much easier to build the proper relationships with your staff and your clients. Having the wrong attitude will spread just as fast as having the right attitude. Your staff and customers will pick up on your personality and if you want to create an exciting and energetic atmosphere, it has to start and end with you.

COMMON SENSE IN PRACTICE

List three things that motivate you.

1. _____

2. _____

3. _____

List three things that really make you angry.

1. _____

2. _____

3. _____

How do you react to people when you are angry?

_____
_____
_____
_____
_____

Are your reactions productive (do they move your relationships forward)? Explain:

_____
_____
_____
_____
_____
_____
_____
_____

What can you do to better control your emotions?

_____
_____
_____
_____
_____
_____

When are your emotions the least under control and the most under control? Order from least (1) to most under control (6)

_____When stressed   _____When angered   _____When at work

_____When tired   _____When at home   _____When on vacation

PASSION: REIGNITE WHAT INSPIRES YOU ABOUT YOUR BUSINESS

I love business because it gives us the ability to create, explore, change, and motivate. Without business there would be no laptops, automobiles, or light bulbs. Shoot! Without business to inspire Columbus to search the seas for better trade routes with India, there would be no America. Business is truly the conduit that moves the world forward.

With today's hectic lifestyle, it is easy to forget the original passion we felt when we first started our business. The monotony of our daily tasks and routines get in the way of our real dreams and desires. Take a moment now to think back about what truly inspires you about your business. What motivated you to start your company? What secret hopes and wishes have defined you?

Yes, I understand; who really has time for such fantasies anymore? There are bills to pay and meetings to attend.   But, with that mindset as your core focus, how long can you maintain the rigors of business before you're simply spent, burnt out, and lost in a sea of uncertainty! Perhaps I am being overly dramatic, but the point is that without purpose for what you do, you will never truly feel successful. It is the passion that first got you started that will fuel your drive to move forward.

It is time that you let your business reinspire you. Passion is not simply a juvenile pursuit: passion will help define your whole business. It is hard to keep going if there is no inner desire to push you forward when the going gets tough. Honestly, I used to think that passion did not matter. I believed that success came from basically pushing the right buttons, not from the illogical pursuit of passion. I realized with the start of my first business just how wrong I was. In fact, I almost lost the company simply because I was not passionate about it. My father and I had just purchased a small juice and smoothie shop with the plan of retooling it into a franchise. We were both excited about the venture. We saw the shop quickly become very successful and we were sure that we could bottle up that success and spread it out nationwide. It did not matter to us that neither one of us liked or regularly drank smoothies; we were after the success, not the passion for the product. We both knew it was a good product, but that was only secondary to us.

Without the passion for the product, we quickly went to work creating what we thought our customers would want, and boy, were we wrong. Within 2 years, we were closing down stores and trying to figure out why our company was not working. One of the biggest problems was that we simply could not relate to our customers. No matter how hard we tried, we never seemed to get the perfect combination of product, price, and atmosphere. Of course, this whole time we were running the company based on the model that we had purchased. Exasperated and frustrated, we finally sat down and asked the tough questions: if we had to start over, what would we build? The conversation ended up being very invigorating as we both passionately laid out what we wanted the company to become. Long story short, we scrapped the old ideas and completely revamped the company's look, product offerings, and business plan. Today people love what we have built. Naturally, we still have many hurdles to overcome in rebuilding the company, but by leading with our passion, we created a concept that people now say is amazing. The best part is that we think it is amazing. It is something that we are now willing to fight for, something we are proud of. Oh, and by the way franchise inquiries are up 200% since we made the change.

If you find yourself simply jumping through the daily hoops associated with your business, it may be time for some change. I am not recommending that everyone completely rebuild their business concept, but I am suggesting that you revisit your own internal concept about why you are in business.

COMMON SENSE IN PRACTICE

What initially caught your interest about the industry that you are in?

_____

_____

_____

_____

What three things get you most excited about your business?

1._____

2._____

3._____

Who is positively affected by your business and how (customers, employees, yourself, etc.)?

_____

_____

_____

_____

_____

What effect would there by on your customers if you were not in business?

_____

_____

_____

_____

_____

Define the absolute best thing about your business:

_____

_____

_____

_____

_____

_____

What are you going to do to share your passion with more people? List at least three action items:

_____

_____

_____

_____

_____

_____

THE MINDSET SOLUTION:

HOCUS POCUS

It drives me crazy how many published books and articles are in the market about how positive thinking is the key to success. It all sounds like Hocus Pocus to me. Success comes from hard work not magical thoughts. The idea that one can will the universe to bring them success by simply thinking it is absurd. Regrettably, my abrasion to the "think happy thoughts" method of doing business has caused me to often miss a key point about business management and leadership.

When I'm being completely honest with myself, I have to admit that mindset matters! This isn't to say that thinking happy thoughts will create success; however, I've learned that mindset dictates your attitude and your attitude dictates your actions. In other words, I came to terms with the fact that if you think you're going to fail, you're more inclined to fail. Or, on the other hand, if you tell yourself you will succeed no matter what, there is a much greater chance of actually being successful. But why? Getting rid of all the Hocus Pocus here is what I think it boils down to. FOCUS. If you're walking around all the time stressed and focused on your worries about failure, you're going to miss key opportunities and make vital mistakes. However, if you're focused on finding solutions and looking for new opportunities, you will always find ways to thrive, grow, and build. Focusing on fear and negativity will stop you dead in your tracks, but focus on the hope of your dreams fulfilled and there will always be a solution to whatever woes are in front of you. Focus on what you can control instead of what you can't.

The mindset solution, as I call it, is really all about reducing stress. We can't operate at peak efficiency when we're stressed. We can't build positive relationships when we're stressed. We certainly can't motivate and inspire those around us when we're stressed. Therefore, it's reasonable to think that if we want to be successful, we must learn how to reduce the stress in our lives. Having the confidence to say with certainty that you will be successful no matter what, comes from having a clear cut plan, the right people in place around you, and the ability to manage your emotions.

FIX YOUR EMERGENCY MODE

Everyone has an emergency mode. For most people, their emergency mode is untrained and causes stress, fear, uncertainty, immobility, and poor decision-making. Some people's emergency modes turn on only in the most severe of circumstances. But, for others, it seems like they are constantly in emergency mode. You know what I'm talking about: everything is a crisis, always rushing around, nothing's ever good enough, and something's always more important than the present moment. People in the never-ending emergency mode tend to believe that they're the only ones that can get anything done, that it is their way or the highway, and that their problems are always more extreme than everyone else's. whether your emergency mode is rarely activated or constantly on, chances are the way you utilize your emergency mode is neither effective nor productive.

Effectively reacting to emergencies (even properly determining what is an emergency) all comes down to effective planning. First, what is an emergency? An emergency is a life- or business-threatening event. How we react to that emergency will dictate whether that event becomes a crisis or simply an unexpected hurdle. Effective emergency management starts by first deciding the level of emergency. Ask yourself: is the event life- or business- threatening? If the answer to this question is no, take a sigh of relief: there is no emergency. Many people treat any unexpected event as an emergency. Stop that! It does not do you or your business any good to over- exaggerate what isn't an emergency.

OK, now that we have averted 90% of our emergencies by simply realizing that they're not an emergency, let's get down to the basics. How do we handle both the real emergencies and the pesky unexpected events the get in the way? There are a few common sense rules that we can learn from people that face real emergencies every single day.

Firemen, police officers and the military all handle extreme situations of life and death with a calm collectiveness. In the heat of the moment, everyone knows their place and exactly what to do. These amazing people are able to accomplish extraordinary feats because they learn to control their emotions, manage their fear, and prepare for whatever comes their way. Their emergency mode helps them perform clear and direct actions with a purpose and a goal. They weren't born heroes, yet they have chosen to live as heroes. Now contrast that to your emergency mode: stress, anger, uncertainty, quick irrational decisions, panic, inability to move forward.

I originally planned to talk about how you should stay out of emergency mode, but upon further examination, I realized that emergencies happen and life gets hard. It is impractical to simply say "stay out of emergency mode." What really needs to happen is a shift in what your emergency mode looks like.

Taking our cues from the amazing men and women who make up our fire, police, and military forces, there are some very helpful tips that we can learn. The first lesson is to be well-trained. For us in the business profession, this means taking every opportunity to read business books, attend seminars and training sessions, and seeking out expert advice from mentors and coaches. Without being trained, how can we expect to handle emergencies properly? It truly is imperative that we take the time to constantly seek out new information about our business and our industry. Training helps prepare us mentally to take on the issues that we face every day. Without training, we won't have the tools and resources necessary to properly handle the things that come our way. Don't ever feel like you have to reinvent the wheel. Learn from those that have gone before and adapt their teaching to your circumstances.

The second lesson is to take what you learn and use it to create plans. The trick to overcoming any emergency is knowing exactly what to do, when to do it, and how to do it. In the business world, this means laying out your policies, practices, values, and expectations. These items will become your action plan. The exercise of writing down your company's best practices and policies isn't so that you can file them away to appease your lawyers. They serve an actual purpose. They are you and your staff's guideline to facing anything that comes your way. I'm not talking about a 50 page dry document that nobody reads, I'm talking about easy to read bullet points that define how your company interacts with the world. Effective emergency management comes from the ability to break down an event or issue into manageable and actionable parts. Without a standard to guide you and your company, even simple unexpected events can become huge emergencies. Knowing exactly how your company will interact with the world will often times avert an emergency before it ever arises.

The third takeaway is that even if your company is a one man shop, you're never alone. Despite the best training and the perfect planning, emergencies can only be tackled through effective teamwork. Don't try to take on the world alone. I'm going to be blunt here...I call it the martyr syndrome, those people who think that they have to take on all the pressures and all the stress alone. Those people who think that they're doing a service by not asking for help. Again, this is a mindset thing. The truth is that the most effective people are those who know how to ask for help and allow others to share their burdens. I don't know if it's pride, lack of confidence, or failure to see the value that others can bring, but the bottom line is that people who think they have to go it alone always fail. A good leader knows that they are only as successful as their team. A good leader relies on their people both in good times and in bad. In business, this means if you have a staff, train them well and then empower them to do their job. See your duty as providing them with the resources necessary for them to complete their tasks. Be your peoples' support line not another hurdle for them to jump over. Then, allow them to be the same for you. If you don't have a staff, you should utilize the support networks of your friends, family, business vendors, coaches, and your industry's organizations. Let the people around you hold you accountable and don't be afraid to let them support you.

The final lesson is to learn how to think solution-oriented not problem-oriented. In my darkest days, whether as a businessman or just a person, I find myself only thinking about all the problems that surround my life. Frankly, this is not healthy or productive. Of course we have problems! That's just life! Remember: problems are not automatically an emergency. Many problems are just small hurdles that we have to overcome. Unfortunately, we quickly promote them to emergency status because we're not thinking about solutions so any issue, big or small, becomes overwhelming. The good news is that if you've already been practicing the above lessons, you're well trained, you have a great plan in place, and a team to support that plan. All that's left is for you to use your resources to solve the problems in front of you. Step one, solve problem one. Step two, solve problem two. Step three…well, you get the idea. The point is whether you're surrounded by everyday issues, or actual life-or business-threatening emergencies, you can't do any better than merely taking on one issue at a time.

Our knee-jerk reaction whenever we're faced with a hurdle is to duck. But this is not the time for hunkering down. This is the time for action. Take each problem, find a solution, act. Easier said than done? Only if that's your mindset, because the reality is that every problem has a solution. However, if you are not willing to take the time (now) to put proper training, procedures, and people in place, the solution may be out of reach. Businesses always seem to get more strategic when in crisis. Unfortunately, by that point, it's often too late.

Part of having the right mindset is taking the time now to prepare for later. The real mindset solution is not found in convincing our inner ego or calling out to the universe. The real mindset solution is being willing to accept that without the proper training, procedures, and people in place, we will be swallowed up by the woes of the world. The real mindset solution realizes that in business, there is no such thing as "going at it alone" or as "just winging it"

COMMON SENSE IN PRACTICE

The first step in fixing your emergency mode is being honest with yourself about how your respond to issues.

Use the space below to summarize your emergency mode (How do you react to emergencies? How quickly/often to you enter into emergency mode? Is your emergency mode effective at solving problems?).

_____
_____
_____
_____

List three things you would like to change about the way you respond to emergencies.

1._____

2._____

3._____

What do you need to accomplish in order to be better prepared and able to respond to issues and emergencies?

_____
_____
_____
_____
_____

In general do you tend to have more of a positive or negative mindset? Explain how your mindset effects your outlook on life and business.

_____
_____
_____
_____

How would you like to see your mindset improve or strengthen?

_____

_____

_____

_____

_____

LOST AND FOUND: A GUIDE TO THE UPS AND DOWNS OF BUSINESS

There is no greater joy as a business owner than to see your sales rise. Your hard work, tenacity, and diligence is all found to be justified the moment that you realize you're beating last month's or last year's sales figures. We all believe and understand that our success comes from proper business planning and superb execution. We're quick to pat ourselves on the back for a job well done. The funny thing is that when things are not going so well, when inevitably we have a streak of down-turned sales, we hardly ever reprimand ourselves. We're eager to tout all the good things as our hard work but, when things don't go right, it is always a poor economy or an untrustworthy staff. Very few of us are actually willing to hold ourselves accountable when our success is fleeing the other direction.

It seems like business is almost fluid, swelling from the tides and winds of the economy. Many businesses believe that they simply have to ride the waves as they come. Others try and build unsinkable organizations, supposedly unaffected by the choppy waters that make up our economy. Those that try to ride the waves seem to always be operating in emergency mode. Success can't be enjoyed or capitalized on because it is too fleeting, and there is a downturn just around the corner to prepare for. On the other hand, those that try and tempt fate by building unsinkable organizations generally end up drowning in huge waves of excuses and denial with no life raft to save them.

The trick to navigating the ebbs and flows of business is first and foremost to love what you do. If you're not passionate about your business, then what motivation will there be when things get a little rough? Business cannot just be about seeking out success: you have to have a reason and a purpose for what you do or else you will be swallowed up by the waves. The second trick is to realize that sales will fluctuate.

The good news is that you can build a business plan in which each upward wave is taller and longer than the downward waves.

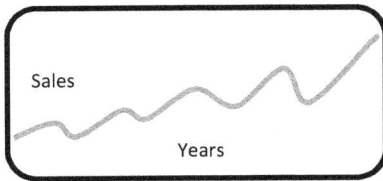

As the graph shows, the idea is to insure that when sales slump, you are still further ahead than you were. You accomplish this by capitalizing on the ups. Sounds like common sense advice but most of us don't follow it. Business is going well, things are busy, and life is looking good. What's the first thing we do? We stop doing the very things that were creating the success. We get too busy to make it to our networking groups, post on Facebook, write our blog, attend chamber meetings, or meet with the advertisers about renewing our marketing campaigns. Next, the friendly little extras we used to do for our customers start getting left out. "It's all good", you tell yourself things are busy and all you have time for is keeping up with the necessities. Of course, victory speeches are best received right after a victory. Don't miss your speech! Capitalize on your success. When you know you are busy and have a crowd, take advantage of that fact. Spend more time, energy, and money promoting yourself (not less). After all, you have the audience: don't wait for everyone to leave before you start your next performance.

As the business owner, your job is to continually grow your business. If you find yourself too busy to continue the activities that originally brought you success, it is time to hire more people. Leverage your success by hiring and empowering your staff to run the operation while you continue your job of bringing in the business. You can also hire someone to go out and do the revenue-generating duties for you, if you would rather manage the daily operations. The main point is just don't stop doing them. It breaks my heart to see successful businesses settle into mediocrity at the first signs of success. The excuse is always the same: "I'm too busy now". Fine. If that is your excuse and mindset, just wait a few months and you will have time again as your pipeline dries up and new leads stop flowing in. I hope you enjoy the ups and downs of your roller coaster business. Just remember, roller coasters are short. They eventually stop and everyone gets off and goes home or over to the next great ride. If you really want to reduce the effects of the ups and downs of business, the key is consistency. Don't stop doing what was working simply because you got busy. Find ways to always provide the same service, value, and quality that originally built your business.

Perhaps most importantly, remember: in order to keep your business growing, you can't be struck dead by fear every time you hit a down slump. Consistency matters. When your sales start dropping, just keep doing what you do best. Don't hide in shame or fear, but keep plowing forward with a confidence that can't be ignored. The moment sales start to drop, many business start cutting expenses and corners to save a buck or two. Ignore this temptation! It only leads to a larger decrease in sales. You need all-systems-go in order to weather the storm. You need your best people and your best resources to quickly drive sales back up. The moment you start cutting is the moment you block your chances of regaining momentum.

HOLD YOURSELF ACCOUNTABLE

Lastly, when sales do slump, don't go looking for excuses and people to blame. First, check yourself. Are you doing everything possible to support the success of your business? What can you change about yourself to become more effective as a leader? What can you change about the way your business operates to make it more efficient? Only after you have examined all of your weaknesses should you start looking at other points in your business to correct, change, or remove.

Don't get me wrong: your staff will make or break your business and if, you have the wrong people in place, you need to act quickly. The concern is that it is simply too easy to point the finger at others. I have found that employers who complain the most about not being able to find good employees also have real problems when it comes to their own management, communication, and expectations. Hands down the best way to increase your ups and decrease your downs is to create an environment that allows your staff to take charge of their job, grow with the company, and be held accountable by a boss who first checks his ego at the door.

COMMON SENSE IN PRACTICE

Describe your gut reactions to a sales drop. Who or what do you normally blame the drop on?

_____

_____

_____

_____

Describe how you normally respond to a sales drop, i.e. do you cut expenses, work longer hours, fire employees, reevaluate your business and sales processes, etc.

_____

_____

_____

_____

Are your gut reactions and responses productive to sales growth? Do you motivate or belittle your staff? Do you rebuild or tear down?

_____

_____

_____

_____

After reading this chapter how will you change the way you operate your business when:

Sales are up?

_____

_____

_____

_____

Sales are down?

_____

_____

_____

_____

FOLLOW THE LEADER:

WHO'S THE LEADER?

Have you ever worked for "that guy"? You know the ego centric, "I love myself so much, I must be a celebrity" attitude. You're afraid to compliment him because his head literally could explode and, at the same time, you would rather watch the company go up in flames than chance questioning his ideas. The sad thing is that the world worships such people. We're told that they are charismatic, great leaders, wonderful people. Of course, the world does not see their dark side. If you're like me, "that guy" could be the reason that now you're the boss. You were pushed too far and decided that you could do better on your own. The problem is that with such a skewed view of leadership in today's society, we quickly become "that guy" to our employees. We're told it's a dog-eat- dog world, and that the best way to succeed is to become everyone else's nightmare.

I would like to go on the record by disagreeing with the world's view of leadership and charisma. Frankly, it's just not a healthy way to live and it is a horrible way to do business. I have had to learn that I am basically not that important. Sure, I do great work, I have risen through the trials, and I helped a lot of people, but that does not make me the center of the universe. I don't even know if that makes me a good person. I think that there is a simpler, more effective version of leadership. I would even go so far as to say that the world's view of leadership is counterproductive. There are three problems that every one of "those guys" (remember, we are those guys) face when trying to operate their business:

1. Ego-first mentality says that it is always someone else's fault. When there is a problem, the attention is put on finding blame rather than solving the problem.

2.   Poor employee morale. Ego-first leaders only celebrate their own success, thus all good things are equated to the boss and all mistakes are equated to the employees. Little victories don't matter and employees get lost in the shuffle of always trying to achieve something bigger than whatever was just accomplished.

3.   No real leader. With the boss self-engaged and otherwise pre-occupied with himself, there is no one at the helm. Decisions are made on a whim, while the boss is high on his own self-image. Deadlines are never realistic and strategy changes every time a new idea bursts into the boss's head.

Obviously, I am exaggerating for drama. Or am I? Let's be honest: we all have someone were thinking of right now. The real question is, if your employees are reading this, are they thinking of you? You can tone it down a notch or two, but at the core, are you the best leader you can be? With so few positive role models to help, we all have a lot to learn in this area. Everyone thinks they know what leadership is. For most of us, leadership is the ability to manage and lead others, an inspiring character, a God-given talent. For me, leadership is so much more.

WHAT IS A LEADER

What is a leader? There is not a one-size-fits-all answer here. True leadership is more about character than any specific action or ability. Leaders can be strong in resolve but meek in stature. They can be firm in conviction but fair with their expectations of others. Most of all, real leaders inspire greatness rather than simply demanding it. There are a few things that every true leader has in common and I feel that the list is in order of importance:

1.   They care about others more than themselves.
2.   They envision greatness in everyone and come alongside you to coax the greatness out.
3.   They understand that their biggest asset are the people around them.
4.   They demand the best first from themselves, then from those around them.
5.   They seek out and desire goals bigger than themselves.

The proof of real leadership is not found merely in actions but in outcomes. Leaders create duplicable results. Their attitude is not "look at what I can do", but focuses more on "look at what you can do". The outcome of this mentality is almost magical in terms of what can be accomplished. When the people who work for real leaders feel valued, safe, and free to grow (even with mistakes made along the way), their creativity, productivity, and loyalty can create an unstoppable organization.

Many would say that you are either born a leader or not. In my opinion, this is not true. Leadership is not based on genetics, but on your ability and willingness to sacrifice enough of yourself to lead. A leader can be anyone who understands that they are not the center of the universe. Leadership is about sacrificing your limelight so that others can shine.

Why is this so important as a business owner? You really only have two options:

1) You build a successful operation tethered to the successful people that you have helped mold and motivate or

2) You take all the credit, trust no one, fly around in circles, live on highs and lows created by success followed by stress. Finally, your engine burns out, but you find that everyone else has taken all the parachutes and left a long, long time ago.

Ask yourself these questions: do find yourself constantly wondering why it is so hard to find good help anymore? Do you find yourself insisting that your business would do better if only your employees would work harder (and longer)? Do you find yourself never satisfied with the quality of the work, but can't really tell people why (you tell yourself you just have this feeling that it's not right)? If you answered yes to any or all of these questions, it is time to reevaluate your management and leadership style. It is time you start focusing on leading your people where you want them to go rather than just complaining that they're not there yet. If you don't make these changes soon, you will eventually fail. This is serious stuff. If you are not willing to take the time to properly communicate your desires, train and instruct your people, and consistently check your own expectations, stress and disappointment will always be at the forefront of your business. Leaders don't make excuses and they don't look for others to blame without first checking their part.

HOW DO YOU BECOME A LEADER?

If we simply believed that you are given leadership abilities based on your genes, then it would be too easy to discount the importance of you actually leading your business. I can't tell you how often I talk with business owners who are struck with fear because of all the problems their business is running into. They can present plenty of reasons for why they are failing but are unable to see any solutions. The first problem is that they are not leading. Maybe they don't listen to the advice of others, maybe they don't empower the right people, and maybe they take on too much, or focus on all the wrong things. It really does not matter because if they would first learn to lead, most of their issues would go away. How? Leaders know how to leverage their strengths with other people's strengths and this builds a stronger business. Sure, there will be problems, but leaders are surrounded by people who can help overcome the problems. When you put your people first, they are allowed to thrive and their skills and abilities will help your organization thrive no matter what comes along. So how do you become a real leader?

1. Care about others more than yourself.
2. Envision greatness in everyone then come alongside them to coax the greatness out.
3. Understand that your biggest asset are the people around you.
4. Demand the best first from yourself, then from those around you.
5. Seek out and desire goals bigger than yourself.

You won't get there overnight: in fact, these skills must be practiced every day for the rest of your life, but you know what they say: practice makes perfect. So start practicing!

COMMON SENSE IN PRACTICE

Name someone who has had a great impact on your life:

_____

How did this person impact you?

_____
_____
_____
_____
_____

What made this person effective?

_____
_____
_____
_____
_____

What person(s) or group(s) have you missed the opportunity to impact?

1._____ 2. _____ 3. _____

What three things can you start doing today to become a better leader?

1._____ 2. _____ 3. _____

GUIDE TO A GREAT RELATIONSHIP
WITH YOUR STAFF

The more managers and business owners I talk to, the easier it becomes for me to believe that employees are the toughest aspect of owning a business. This is an odd concept for me because employees are supposed to make life easier and more productive. Yet, I constantly hear how small business owners wish they could do it all without employees. Like so many other aspects of business, we have believed the lie that management is complicated and that you can't do it without years of higher educational study. However, I would argue that managing employees is the best part of business ownership. It is something that we should embrace, and it is something that can be easily explained in just three words: "Employees are people!" I know, no real innovation there, but think about it in the simplest of terms: what do people want? whether they are your customers, your employees, or your friends, people want to be treated fairly and with respect.

Master this one rule and you will have a great relationship with your staff, your customers, and all those around you. Again, people want to be treated fairly and with respect. "Manager" is really a poor term for the boss. A better word is "Motivator." As the boss, your job is to motivate your employees (sorry, "people"). The people in your life are your partners. Customers partner with you to purchase your products or services. Your friends and family partner with you to keep you accountable. Your staff partners with you to grow your business. Once you can begin to see your staff as partners, the whole relationship dynamics change. You now realize that you rely on them just as much as they rely on you. Treat them fairly and with respect and you will have the best staff in the world.

COMPENSATION

Obviously an employee/employer partnership is based around the employee performing duties for pay. But it is more than that. Your employees will make or break your business so you need to insure that you are hiring the right people and setting a strong standard from day one. The best way to accomplish both of these goals is to have a compensation plan that rewards employees for working with you and partnering to grow your business. It is my belief that compensation plans should be based on a paid-for-performance system, meaning that all new employees working at the same job and tasks should be started at the same rate and rewarded with raises based on how well they perform their job. The temptation is to reward raises based on longevity to try to increase retention rates. At first glance, this plan makes sense: if you stay, we pay. This cuts down on training new employees and can make for a better-run operation by keeping senior employees who do not need much supervision. However, automatic annual raises can demotivate employees because they begin to expect them. Thus, there is no sense of urgency to perform well. Simply encouraging employees to stick around for their annual raise may not be the best thing for the business. By rewarding raises for exceptional performance, it is easy to create a competitive atmosphere that keeps employees motivated.

One potential issue with pay-for-performance strategy, however, is that pay can be more variable across employees. You can have multiple employees who all have been with the organization for the same amount of time all making different amounts of money. Thus, if the pay raise process is not fully understood, the compensation plan may seem unfair or unjust to employees. The best way to prevent that, and actually insure that the compensation plan works to motivate employee performance, is to make sure that employees fully understand the process. You need to have written clear-cut goals and expectations that must be met in order to be eligible for a raise. As we will talk about below, "clear-cut" also has to be attainable. If you keep your compensation plan too complicated, it will not work to motivate your employees. In fact, it will discourage them from even trying to work harder. A clear-cut compensation plan really should fit into the mold below:

- Job description to outline specific duties and expectations

- Expectation Statement to outline company principles and work ethic standards

- Company Goals to inform employees about the company's purpose and growth plans

- Detailed training program and employee orientation

- Ongoing coaching and instruction

- Regular six month evaluation

If you have each one of these requirements in place, I guarantee you that your employees will be easier to manage, happier and more productive. Unfortunately, if you take out just one of the requirements the whole plan implodes.

STARTING PAY

Many businesses struggle with where to start their new employees, especially hourly employees. A strong temptation for small business owners is to start at their state's minimum wage as an hourly rate and reward raises from there. However, I have found businesses that start at minimum wage have higher turnover rates and complain about not being able to attract quality employees. Employers must look at what the position is worth in terms of its potential to help or hinder success and pay accordingly. If employers can create a compensation plan that represents the importance of the position, they will be more likely to attract the right person. For example, hourly employees in the service and retail sector are the primary contact between the organization and the customers. This means that if employees are not representing the company well, the customers will have no other perspective to judge their experiences. Because businesses must rely on a strong and study stream of loyal customers, they must have employees with the skills and work ethic to represent their organization with respect and professionalism. It is too easy to discount the importance of hourly employees, while the truth of the matter is that hourly employees will make or break the success of almost any business.

The same is true for salaried staff. The lower you pay, the lower the quality of person you will attract. Also, most people willing to accept low pay are not looking for a partnership: they are looking for something to hold them over until the next thing comes along and they will bring that attitude with them. The highly motivated, highly committed employees won't even consider a job if they know it pays too low. Today, it is easy to find compensation bench marks, but I would also just give it the crap test. If you were in your employee's shoes, would you say "oh crap," or would you be excited to work for you, based on the benefits and growth potential offered? Perhaps most importantly is to avoid thoughts such as "when I was in your shoes." Remember inflation? What you were happy to get even just 10 years ago is now change in the bucket. Bottom line: if you can't afford to pay fairly, you are not ready to hire for that position yet. And that is ok. The last thing you want to do is stretch yourself too thin trying to grow too fast.

WHERE DOES MOTIVATION COME FROM?

Many businesses expect that an employee's need to receive a paycheck will manage the employee's behavior. This is simply not true. Compensation plans must reward behavior that creates success; pay is not the primary management tool. The proper training, coaching, support, and technology all need to be in place in order for employees to meet the organizational goals. If managers are not actively managing their employees through constant coaching, most employees will not reach the level in which a pay raise is acceptable. Employees will quickly become frustrated if they are constantly passed up for a raise but never told why.

Managers or small business owners must be active participants in their employee's success because their employees are active participants in the business' success (or failure). Good compensation plans must line up with the business plan and strategies. Managers or small business owners must look at their employees as success partners and align their business goals with the employee's compensation plan. The great thing about pay-for-performance strategies is that variable pay allows employees to be rewarded when their work causes the company success, but also does not hold the company to high, fixed salaries that they can't afford if sales fall.

IS YOUR COMPENSATION PLAN PERCEIVED AS FAIR?

Ultimately, the success of a compensation plan comes down to how it is perceived by employees. If the plan is consistent, easy to understand, and attainable, it is more likely to be seen as fair, even if the pay is lower than some competitors. Employees often judge if their pay is fair by taking into account their work load versus their pay, and their pay in comparison to their peer's pay that have similar skills and responsibilities. If employees see any inequality with their pay, they will try and correct it by not working as hard or looking for a better paid position with a different organization.

When looking into how you pay your employees, it is important to remember that attracting and keeping quality employees will keep you on track to meet your own business goals. Begin by starting with a pay structure that will encourage quality employees to apply. Then, continue the successful relationship by presenting opportunities for your employees to grow with you.

COMMON SENSE IN PRACTICE

If you had no employees, would your business still be able to function as successfully? Explain why or why not:

_____
_____
_____
_____
_____

Is your relationship with your employees positive or stressful? _____

What three things could you do to better your relationship with your employees?

1._____ 2. _____ 3. _____

What three things would you like your employees to do better?

1._____ 2. _____ 3. _____

Use the space below to outline how you can become more involved with your employees to help them succeed at the three things you listed above.

_____
_____
_____
_____
_____
_____

SETTING YOUR EMPLOYEES

UP FOR SUCCESS

One of the biggest complaints I hear from business owners is that they just can't get their employees to take full ownership of their jobs. These owners all seem to make the same assumption: "My employees should feel just as passionate about the business as I do." This assumption is generally promptly followed by the assumption that "My employees should be willing to do whatever it takes to make the business successful."

Just stop right there. Hold your horses! You're the owner, you're the boss. That means that your priorities and your employee's priorities are not automatically the same. As the boss, it is your job to set your employees up for success. Most people make the assumption that employees will naturally want to see their employer succeed. The fact of the matter is that an employee's mind set is completely different from yours as the owner. Employees come on board because they need a job to pay their bills and fund the activities (outside of work) that are important to them. To you, your business is your life. You have invested everything into it. To your employees, it is just a day job. Starting out with the expectation that your employees will care as much as you do just sets both of you up for failure and disappointment.

A good employee will naturally want to please you and do a good job, but that does not mean that you both have the same goals. It is your job to set strong expectations, provide clear direction, and align your employee's success with the goals of the business. Remember, from the employee's perspective the success of the company is in your hands. They are simply responsible for the tasks and duties that you pay them to perform. If you are not getting what you want or need out of your employees, 8 times out of 10 it is because you have not properly told them what you expect or, frankly, because your expectations are out of line with the reality of the employee/employer partnership. Let me point out a few misconceptions that many business owners have about their employees commitment. Your employees do not want to work late every night. Your employees don't understand why you underpay them and overwork them. Your employees do not feel that their life's calling is to work for you. Most importantly, your employees are not motivated if they are not empowered to fully complete the tasks that you pay them to do.

All this is not to say that there is no such thing as a mismatched employee: there are just some people who aren't willing to learn or follow expected guidelines. However, if you find yourself constantly frustrated by your employees, I would boldly suggest that you review your own expectations and management techniques. Ask yourself (and be honest), the following questions:

- Are your expectations fair (meaning realistic, attainable with the resources available, reasonable based on the pay and skill level of your employees, etc.)?

- Have you effectively communicated your expectations?

- Do you provide the tools and resources to allow your staff to meet your expectations?

- Is your compensation plan tied to your expectations (in other words, do you reward good behavior)?

- Do you regularly review the expectations with your employees?

- Do you regularly give feedback (both positive and constructive) to help employees meet your expectations?

The above list is really pass or fail. If you find yourself lacking on any one of the above points, your employees will never meet your standards. An employee can only be as strong and effective as their manager and, if you are neglecting your duties as manager, your business will suffer. If you want motivated, engaged, and committed employees, then you must be a motivated, engaged, and committed manager.

MANAGING EMPLOYEES

Managing employees can be rough for a small business. Most likely, you are team leader, department manager and CEO, not to mention head of HR and payroll. How does a small business manager find time to instruct, motivate, and supervise while also having time to manage the books, customers, and projects? More times than not, small business owners begin to neglect their management duties as "more pressing" issues quickly overrun their daily activities.

Being the boss quickly becomes simply expecting everyone to do their job. This is not a bad expectation, but the underlying tone becomes that you don't care. Employees begin to feel that their job is not vital to the success of the organization and their performance starts to drop. As employees' performance begins to waver, you work harder to pick up the slack, further diminishing your ability to properly manage. This never-ending cycle would drive anyone crazy, but it can be prevented!

HIRE TO REDUCE YOUR WORKLOAD

A new hire should always reduce your personal workload. You hire someone because you get to a point where your time can be more productive elsewhere. That means that the new hire should free up your time, not bog it down. Take the time at the beginning to properly train your new employees and continue to invest a few minutes every day in their lives and work. Taking time out to manage your employees will help them become more productive, which in turn will help you become more productive (and successful).

MAKE SURE EVERYONE IS ON THE SAME PAGE

It is too easy to get busy and have everyone running in different directions. It is vitally important no matter what your business is to have weekly (or at least monthly) meetings with your whole staff. These meetings should be used to update employees on projects, answer questions, train and motivate, and remind everyone about your company's overall vision. Be open with your employees and ask for their impute and advice. This is also a great time to thank your staff for their hard work.

HELP YOUR EMPLOYEES TAKE OWNERSHIP OF THEIR WORK

Nothing demotivates an employee more than not seeing a direct correlation between what they do and the organization's mission and goals. Help each employee see and understand that what they are doing affects everyone around them, including their own success. Take this one step further and reward those employees whose hard work has made the company more successful. The key here is to not hand out random bonuses or raises. This just frustrates employees, as they tend to see "random" raises as favoritism.

Set up a well-defined reward system so that employees know exactly what they need to do for the company in order to receive the raise or bonus.

CHANGE YOUR MINDSET ABOUT EMPLOYEES

Many small business owners fail to realize the power and importance of their employees. Small business employees should be treated as entrepreneurs right alongside you, the owner. You may be taking a risk on them but they are also taking a risk on you. Treat them as business partners. Value their time and their work. Most importantly, realize that you can't be successful without them. If you don't take the time to properly train, coach, and motivate your employees, your business's full potential will never be met. Remember that investing in your employees both with your time and your money is also investing in the future of your business.

COMMON SENSE IN PRACTICE

How well do your employees understand your company's mission, goals, and objectives? Check only one.

__ They only understand their job function

__ They understand the underlying company mission/culture as it relates to their job function

__ Company culture is very important, but it is more about unwritten rules and camaraderie

__ All employees are taken through an orientation about the company's values and mission

__On top of new employee orientation, company culture is used to consistently motivate, reward, and manage

In one word or phrase describe the value of your employees in terms of current and future success: _____

What three things could you do to better educate your employees?

1._____ 2. _____ 3. _____

What three things can you do to better motivate your employees?

1._____ 2. _____ 3. _____

List six action items that you can do or put in place to help your employees succeed.

1. _____ 2. _____ 3. _____

4. _____ 5. _____ 6. _____

Mark Zarr

How will implementing these six action items make you more successful?

_____
_____
_____
_____
_____
_____
_____
_____
_____
_____
_____
_____

DON'T PUT YOUR MARKETING

IN A SHOTGUN

When I opened my first store, I was extremely excited to start marketing. My ego was 10 feet tall and ready to take on the world. I wanted to see my company's name everywhere. I was on the radio, TV, newspapers, magazines, coupon books, and websites. I figured with all the marketing I was doing, success would be practically guaranteed. Nine months and over $50,000 later, lost somewhere in the world of media advertising, I decided that marketing did not work. Nine months earlier, there was not an advertiser that I did not love (and they all loved me). However, I soon realized that even though my store's name was everywhere, success was not being drawn toward me. Sales were way below projections and my customer base was not getting any larger. I sat in my office scratching my head. My degree had focused heavily on marketing, and should have taught me everything I needed to know. I was doing everything right out of the textbook. Why wasn't it working? I was advertising with the same tools that all the big dogs were using. If it worked for the big "expert" corporations, why was it not working for me?

Years later, I hear this same complaint from many small businesses. It seems like the one thing that most small businesses can agree on is that marketing does not work. To some extent, this is true. People are bombarded with advertisements everywhere. Consumers are surrounded by countless numbers of messages, images, and voices. This makes it appear almost impossible to be heard among the clamor. For years, the solution to this problem has been what I call shotgun marketing. The idea is if you show up in enough different places, something is bound to get someone's attention. A shotgun never misses, right? Wrong!

I used a shotgun for the first time as a young teenager. I was full of confidence as I aimed at the target less than 25 yards away. I pulled the trigger and when the smoke cleared, I was on my back and the target sat there, taunting me, unaffected by my attempt to destroy it. After that experience, I moved my attention to a .22 rifle with a scope. A lot less firepower, but the gun fit my size and skill level, allowing me to hit my target almost every time and from even greater distances.

Targeted marketing is a fancy term that advertisers have started to throw around to represent today's technological ability to market to defined demographics. These new technologies can be very useful, but it opens up a whole new set of questions. Who do I target? What should I target them with? What I end up seeing most often is a hybrid form of targeted-shotgun marketing. You pick a target market and then randomly fire at them with different arsenals, hoping one will stick.

Let's take a step back and stop marketing with war tactics. Our customers, both potential and current, are not targets, they are allies. We don't want to aim anything at them-they'll just duck. Effective marketing invites customers to participate in your business. We want to build partnerships, not hit lists. All right, enough with the analogies! What really matters to any business is action. Terminology and strategy is only as effective as it is usable. The root of any marketing strategy boils down to a need to increase sales. Let's start there.

There are three primary ways to increase sales:

1. Increase the number of customer you have
2. Increase the frequency of your customers purchases
3. Increase the average ticket price (upsell)

When most people think of marketing, they think in terms of increasing their number of customers. Unfortunately, this is also the hardest, least predictable, and most expensive way of marketing. Large organizations spend millions of dollars per year marketing to new customers. However, small businesses do not have these kinds of budgets and must find alternative ways to increase their sales.

College marketing courses teach that a "Target Market" is defined as a demographical and/or geographical group of the overall population who is most likely to purchase your product. These courses instruct you to find your "Target Market" and cater an advertising campaign to that market. Say what? Time for a real world reality check! For years I lived by this rule, and I almost died by it. I knew exactly who my customers should be; the problem was that I could not attract, them no matter what I tried. Eventually, I realized that my Target Market was not a demographical and or geographical group of the overall population. My Target Market was my current customers, the people interested in my product, and the people that already knew who I was. These current customers would make or break my business. Plus, I had easy access to them. It would not take a lot to market to them.

College Marketing Class Model   Real World Marketing Model

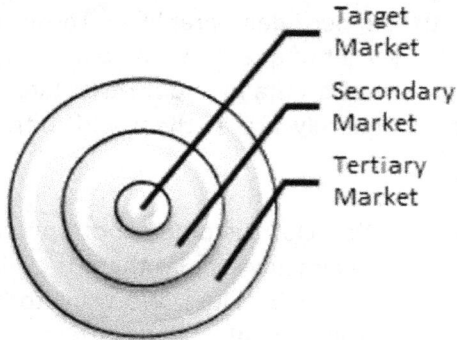

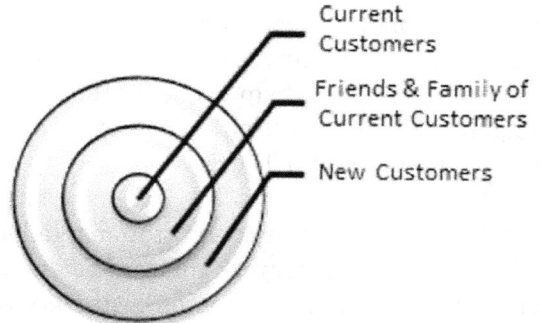

MARKETING STRATEGY

Marketing to your current customers is a great way to quickly and cost-effectively increase your sales. You don't want to start nickel-and-dimming your current customers and you should not raise your prices unless you have to, but there are other ways to partner with your current customers.

BRING MORE VALUE TO YOUR CUSTOMERS

Upselling is the most effective way to quickly increase sales. Most business owners don't upsell because they think it means misleading their customers into purchasing more than they need. The key to upselling is creating ways to bring more value to your current customers. Instead of trying to sell them something they don't need or want, find ways to make what they are currently interested in even better. For example, let's say that you own a coffee shop and you make a $1 profit anytime you upsell an extra shot or pastry. Now, let's say you average 300 customers a day and only a third of them accept your upsell offer. You will have increased your net profits by $100 per day. This is approximately $3,000 per month in additional profits without spending a dime on marketing! Even if you only get 15% to accept the offer, what could your business do with an extra $1,500 per month? This same concept can be used no matter what industry you are in. If you own a marketing firm and someone purchases a website design, upsell them a hosting package for $25 a month. With just 8 upsells, you increase your revenue on a reoccurring bases by $200 per month. You get the idea.

KEEP THEM COMING BACK

Today's technology makes it easy to stay in touch with your customers. Facebook® is a great start. Just create a free Facebook® page then print a couple of posters for your countertop, asking your customers to "like" you to get great deals. You can do the same thing with email newsletters and inexpensive text marketing programs. Even your receipt can be a marketing tool-have the receipt print out a coupon valid for the next 3 days. Send out email coupons for buy one, get one free discounts (now your customers are bringing their friends and family to you. They are marketing for you!). Look at the coffee shop again for another example of just how easy and effective these tools can be:

If we assume that the coffee shop's average customer comes in once a week and purchases a $4 espresso, what would it look like if just an eighth of them started coming in twice a week? The coffee shop currently gets around 2100 visitors a week. One eighth of 2100 is 262 more visits per week. Even if we have to discount the additional sale by a dollar to get the customer to come back, that is still $786 in additional revenue per week. And that is assuming that your FREE marketing is only 12.5% effective. When you add this to the additional profits from the upsells, you have increased your monthly sales by over $6000 for free or very little cost. Reinvest half of that into advertising to bring in new customers and you are on your way to steady growth.

The lesson here is to market first to your current customers. They are the ones listening. They are the ones that care about what you have to say. New customer growth can then be built from the increase in profits created by partnering with your existing clientele.

COMMON SENSE IN PRACTICE

What kind of marketing have you tried? Check all that apply.

__ Radio   __ Coupon book or mailer

__ TV   __ Other _____

__ Print (Newspaper, Magazine, etc.)

What is your most effective means of advertising? _____ (Keep doing this).

What is your least effective means of advertising? _____ (Stop doing this).

Explain how you measure effectiveness.

_____
_____
_____

Describe the desired outcomes of your marketing.

_____
_____
_____

Describe how marketing to your current customers would help you reach your desired marketing outcomes.

_____
_____
_____
_____

Brainstorm as many different ways as you can think of to market to your current customers (i.e. upsell products, offer a newsletter, come back soon coupons, Facebook fan page, etc.)

_____

_____

_____

_____

_____

_____

_____

Pick three of the items from the above list that you can start implementing right away.

1._____ 2. _____ 3. _____

THE SOCIAL MEDIA EFFECT: OVERHYPED OR NEW ERA?

"Hello big wide world"…" Hey, where is everyone?"

We all know that we need to leverage social media sites such as Facebook, LinkedIn, and YouTube. The problem is that most of us don't know why we need to or how we are supposed to make the social media magic work. We create a username and password, throw up a few lines for our profile, make a couple of posts, then wait for the world to find us. What must of us don't realize is that social media can actually be a very lonely place. When it comes to social media, most of us twiddle our thumbs and listen to the crickets chirp, all the while hearing success stories of businesses booming because of social media.

I have to admit that I was a late adapter to the whole Facebook and social media craze. For the longest time, I refused to see the movement as anything more than a bunch of egotistical kids who thought people actually cared about what they were doing at any and every given moment of the day. For those of you who still see Facebook in that light, get over it! Social media is the new face of the Internet (no pun intended). It is no longer only about Google and Yahoo! searches. The internet may have made everyone an expert, but social media has made them stars. If I wanted my business to grow, I knew that I also had to become a star.

The same is true for your business. More and more people are starting to use Facebook to search for businesses instead of traditional internet search engines. That means that if you don't have a Facebook page, you don't exist to thousands of potential customers. The real power of social media is that it is free. Businesses used to be constrained by what they could afford. Today, any business can compete alongside multinational organizations. Not only can you compete, but you can win. Facebook, LinkedIn, Twitter, and YouTube have leveled the playing field. The old saying that time is money has come true. Advertising budgets, through social media, are only limited by the amount of time that you have to spend on them. The rewards for your time can be increased sales, better brand awareness, customer loyalty, and so much more. Yes, I hear you. You know the potential is out there but the task is daunting. Many people think that social media success is pure luck (and in some cases, this is true), but capturing your share of the pie has to be calculated. Just like your website, and your physical place of business, you can't simply build it and believe that they will come. It takes time, commitment, skill, and trial and error to make your business work: social media is no different.

YOUR BRAND

As I said earlier, I was late to the social media party, but once I launched my Facebook page for my smoothie and espresso chain, I immediately got a great response. I picked up over a thousand fans in just a few weeks. Not bad for someone who had no idea what they were doing. However, what I had done was stumbled upon the first rule of Facebook. Your fan page is only as strong as your brand. I got to capitalize on the fact that I already had thousands of customers across the western United States. Fans were already looking for me on Facebook so, once I showed up, it was easy to convert them to likes. The most important rule to remember is that Facebook is a tool to continue your brand. You can't simply create a Facebook brand. You should use social media to promote what you are already doing. You already have to have some substance to your organization. Don't worry if you are a startup; I am not saying that you should wait before creating your page. I am, however, saying that in order to be liked on Facebook, you have to be liked in real life. You have to have a relevant message that people want to be a part of. Your Facebook and other social media pages need to back up your brand. The best pages focus on your passions, your "why" statements. Your page should tell everyone not what you sell, but why you sell it.

ENGAGE AND PARTICIPATE

At its core, social media is...well, SOCIAL. That means that you have to be actively engaged in it. For example, with Facebook, you need to explore the pages of other businesses and organizations (especially ones that complement what you are selling) and comment on their posts. Also, use your page to talk about relevant news or information that relates to your products. Use your page to really establish yourself as an expert in your industry.

Many people make the mistake of running around all over Facebook promoting themselves or their product. Remember, Facebook is social. The same rules apply on Facebook as at a party with friends, coworkers, and acquaintances. At a party, you might use your expertise to share interesting information about your industry, but you won't get invited to the next one if all you do is tell people all night long that they have to check out your business. In order to be effective on Facebook, you have to have conversations. You can't simply hand people your business cards.

Just like a party, you have to invite people to show up. Who should you start with? Your friends and family; just like any party, you want your core group to be involved. They are the ones that are going to say great things about you and help share your message with others. If you don't have any real friends on Facebook, it is going to be very hard to meet new friends. Again, normal social rules apply here. In real life, you are introduced to new people through those you already know. The next groups of people that you want to invite are your current customers. Again, for the same reasons that you would invite friends and family, you need a good group of loyal people surrounding you before you will attract new customers.

Facebook is not about marketing to new customers. Just so that we are on the same page, let me say that again: Facebook is not about marketing to new customers. It is about building relationships and partnerships that can help turn more people on to your products and services. You need and want your current customers all over your Facebook page. Invite your current customers by putting up a poster in your store asking people to like you on Facebook and follow you on Twitter, add like and follow links to your website and emails; put a little note in the bag with your customer's purchases. Whatever it takes, you have to get the word out to your customers.

Facebook does offer advertising services and it is important to mention that it is a great tool, but it is not a replacement to being actively engaged. Use Facebook advertising only after you have mastered being a participant. One other way to directly promote your products on Facebook is to give stuff away. Once you have a fan base of over 300 people, it makes sense to start giving product or services away to highlight what you offer. You can use Facebook to create surveys, contests, and polls to base your giveaways around. Just remember that it is all about creating interaction. Don't just randomly pick a fan; get people involved on your page with the giveaways. Be creative and have fun.

MORE THAN FACEBOOK

I primarily focused on Facebook because it is, by far, the most effective social media platform. But that does not mean that you should neglect the others. Be a part of as many social sites as you have time for. The great thing is that there are many tools to link all the platforms together. Which means you only have to post a few places. This works for things like Twitter and LinkedIn, but keep Facebook a standalone task. Other must-do social media platforms are:

- LinkedIn: This is a very professional networking site. You must have a LinkedIn account because it is a great way to network with other professionals. Just make sure you keep your posts relevant to the business world.

- Twitter: Honestly, I am still not a huge fan of Twitter. But is still I use it as handy way to post links to my blogs, events, and other information that I want people to know about. Just don't start telling people what you are doing every 10 minutes, PLEASE.

- Blog: Today it is almost imperative that you have a blog. You should try to integrate it into your website, but there are a ton of free blogs on the market. WordPress (which also allows you to make great websites at little or no cost, and with very little experience. NO CODE: YEA!), Blogger, Hub Pages, and more. I would really recommend WordPress. While you are at it, you can move your whole website over. The key with a blog is to keep it short, relevant and informative, post at least once a week, and put the link to the post on Facebook, Twitter, and LinkedIn. Don't forget that a blog should inform people about relevant information, not sell to them! For example, if you own a greenhouse, write a blog about gardening, not about your products.

- YouTube: This is great for a variety of purposes: post a weekly video blog (1-2 minutes), create a funny and entertaining 30-second commercial, post a video from an event you hosted, etc. The key to success with YouTube is that it has to be short, and it has to be entertaining. Of course, post the YouTube link on all your other social media accounts.

No matter how you decide to leverage your social media, it is important that we keep our eye on the big picture. Social media is not hard, just follow normal social rules. Keep your information relevant and entertaining. Lastly, engage your fans and followers in order to build relationships. Oh right, and have fun! Remember, that to get likes you have to be liked.

COMMON SENSE IN PRACTICE

What Social Media do you currently use? Check all that apply.

__ Facebook   __ LinkedIn

__ Twitter   __ Other _____

__ YouTube

Why do you use social media?

_____
_____
_____

How do you currently use social media (i.e. to communicate with customers, promote a blog, advertise new products, etc.)?

_____
_____
_____

Do you have any preconceived ideas, negative or positive, about social media?

_____
_____
_____
_____
_____
_____

Explain what you will do to overcome the negative preconceived ideas you have.

_____

_____

_____

_____

_____

_____

_____

Brainstorm all the different ways that you can use social media to stay connected with your customers.

_____

_____

_____

_____

_____

_____

_____

Pick three of the items from the above list that you can start implementing right away.

1._____ 2. _____ 3. _____

IF A TREE FALLS IN A DESERTED FOREST DOES IT MAKE A SOUND? INSURE THAT YOUR MESSAGE IS HEARD

It does not matter how much money you spend on marketing if there is no one around to listen to your message. In today's media-oversaturated world, there is really no risk of sending your message to a deserted forest. However, if you don't have the right message, and if you're not talking to the right people, you just as well could be lecturing to an empty hall. The problem is that there are so many voices competing for attention that most people can't focus on any one falling tree long enough for its message to become clear.

Most business owners assume that they know who their customers are and what they want. Regrettably, many business owners don't have a clue. I learned the hard way that it is too easy to assume that the reasons you like your product are the same reasons that your customers like your products. This assumption can often lead to disaster. If you want your message to be heard, the first step is to understand who your customers are and what they want.

SURVEY YOUR CUSTOMERS

The art of asking questions (the right questions) really seems to be fading fast from the world of small business. I am a huge advocate of surveys, but today's surveys never ask the important questions. They stick with superficial questions like, "Rate your experience on a scale of 1-10." This really only tells you if people are happy or unhappy, but it fails to ask the critical question of "why?"

Simply knowing how your customer feels will do nothing to help you understand who your customers are and what they care about. A good survey will ask direct questions and often times lead to surprising results.

How can a survey help you build a better message? One example was found when I conducted a survey on the customers of my smoothie chain. From the time that we opened our first store, we decided that our "Primary Target Customer" would be families. We catered everything, from the atmosphere of our stores through our marketing message, to attract families. When I conducted the survey, I asked people's age range, marital status, and number of children. I dove even deeper and asked how often they brought their family in to our stores. The results were business changing. Less than 12% of our customers had children, and fewer than 30% of those families bought smoothies with their kids. The real eye opener of this survey was just how dead wrong we were about who our customers actually were. We were so sure that the majority of our customers were young mothers with their children. However, most of our customers were mixed between college kids (of both sexes) and middle aged business professionals. The revelation was that we had predefined who are customers should be then only noticed the customers that fit our definition. It is kind of like when you buy a new car and you think yours is so unique, until you purchase it, and you see it all over the place. Our minds only show us what we are looking for.

That is why it is so important to ask direct questions and then be open to the answers. Based on the survey, we eventually changed our whole business model and started targeting our message to our actual customers. Our inability to ask the right questions had caused us to focus on the wrong people, with the wrong message. Even after we knew all the right answers, it still took some time to pivot our business model around the new information. The information contradicted our vision and our dream for the business, and this was a hard thing to overcome.

TIME TO CHANGE GEARS

Every business started with a dream or a moment of inspiration, and with someone's sweat equity and ingenuity. The idea of business, of selling ones goods or services, has been around since the beginning of time. I suppose that means that businesses have also seen failure from the beginning of time. Some poor entrepreneur in the stone age invested all of his rocks into selling "Dinosaur-on-a-stick" to wandering nomads passing by. Of course, as is true with all great ideas before their time, Dinosaur-on-a-stick failed to draw enough attention and the owner had to close down his cave and join back into the ranks of nomadic scavengers.

So why do seemingly good ideas fail? The problem does not start with the idea. It may not even start with the application of the idea. The problem starts with the dream. Dreams are wonderful at providing inspiration, but they can also lock us into an inevitable downward spiral. The problem with dreams is that they tie us to specific expectations and emotions about how our business (dream) should operate. When reality gets in the way of those expectations, we hold on to the exact dream rather than the essence of the dream. The reality is that the moment a great business idea is launched, the constraints of the real world start to interfere.

Let's take our caveman entrepreneur, for example. His dream was to sell Dinosaur-on-a-stick from his cave. The dream dictated that he would sell his product from his cave as people passed by. The problem was that not enough people were passing by. His dream told him that he had to sell Dinosaur-on-a-stick from his cave to constitute success. However, if he would have taken the essences of his dream and adapted it to the constraints of reality, he would have realized that following the nomads and setting up a tent to sell his products to the hungry and worn out tribe every evening would have kept him in business.

We get so attached to our dream's image that once we start seeing any form of defeat, we emotionally hunker down. What we should do is look for innovative solutions, even if they don't conform to our exact expectations. Successful business has to be adaptable. A profitable business takes a great idea and then molds it to fit the needs and constraints of reality and the current business environment.

Dreams are powerful starting points, but in order to create lasting success, you must take the essence of the dream and figure out how to use it to inspire an ever-evolving process. Pluck the inspired ideas out of the dream and place them on a well thought out plan. Make your dream's ideas the focus of your plan, but don't let your dream overtake the concept of turning a profit. The dream is your starting point but you will find that you have to let parts of it go so that the ideas can be adapted, sharpened, and, most importantly, profitable.

HOW TO ASK THE RIGHT QUESTIONS

Creating a powerful and useable survey means that you ask questions that will help drive your strategy. Surveys are not just for marketing purposes; they also insure that your in-store message is effective. They should help you answer questions such as:

• Does customer service match up with my mission and value statement?

• Is my product/service as good as I think it is?

• Where can my product/service improve?

- Who uses my product or service?

- Why do people use my product or service (price, quality, convenience, etc.)?

An effective survey should be direct, concise, and easy to complete. There should be no more the 10 questions, and each one should have defined answers to choose from (yes/no, scale, multiple choice). You can't quantify a bunch of short essay answers (it is ok to add a place for comments at the end, if you want).

Asking the right questions is really the hard part. You will need to spend some time thinking about what you actually want to know then drill down to the core. For example don't ask people to rate your customer service. Instead, pick two or three actual elements of your customer service (i.e. ask if customers are greeted with a smile, or ask if their questions were fully answered, or if they would recommend you to their friend based on their experience).

See the chart below for more examples of how to drill down to the right question.

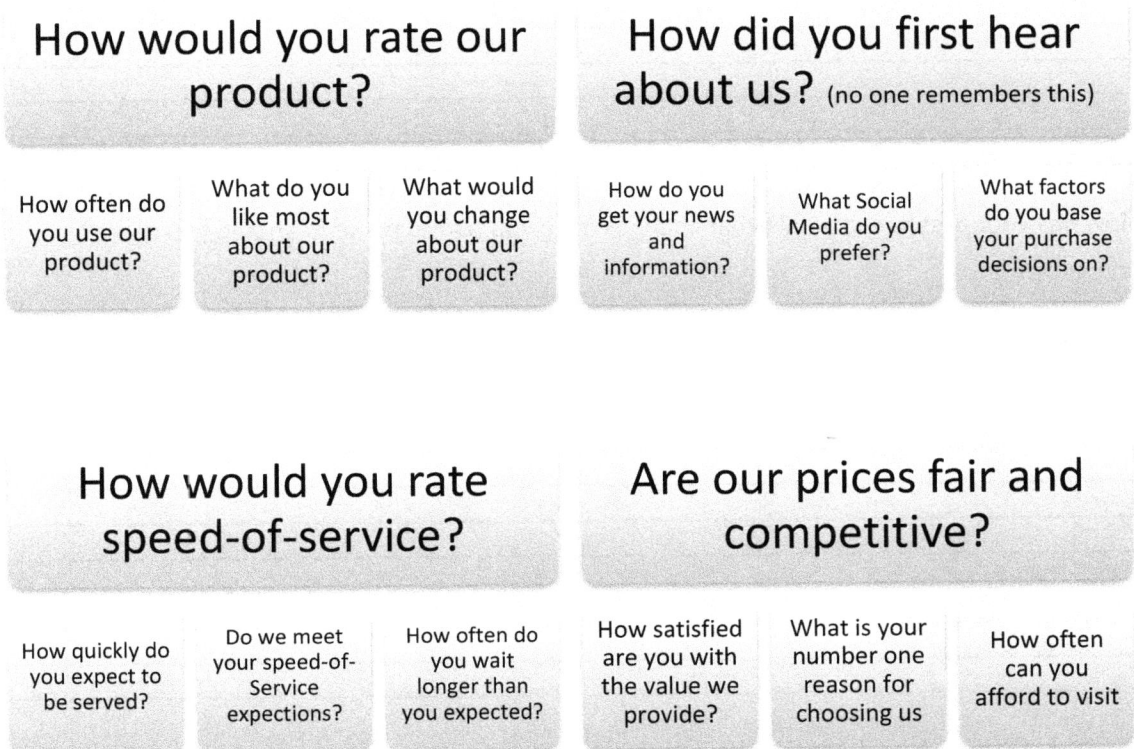

How would you rate our product?

| How often do you use our product? | What do you like most about our product? | What would you change about our product? |

How did you first hear about us? (no one remembers this)

| How do you get your news and information? | What Social Media do you prefer? | What factors do you base your purchase decisions on? |

How would you rate speed-of-service?

| How quickly do you expect to be served? | Do we meet your speed-of-Service expections? | How often do you wait longer than you expected? |

Are our prices fair and competitive?

| How satisfied are you with the value we provide? | What is your number one reason for choosing us | How often can you afford to visit |

COMMON SENSE IN PRACTICE

Describe the original dream that started your business.

_____
_____
_____
_____
_____
_____
_____
_____
_____
_____
_____
_____
_____
_____
_____

How has your dream evolved? What changes have you had to make or should you make?

_____
_____
_____
_____
_____
_____
_____
_____
_____
_____
_____
_____

Create a Survey. Use the boxes below, as in the example from this chapter. Start by stating the big picture question then drill down and create two or three targeted questions that will help answer your big picture questions. The targeted questions will actually be the questions in your survey.

DON'T SELL

YOURSELF SHORT

It is interesting to me that colleges and universities don't teach sales techniques. During my studies for my MBA not one class focused on or even mentioned the need for selling. This is odd because after being in business for many years, I have come to realize that nothing moves forward without sales. Take any business in any industry and at its core, you will always find the business motivated, sustained, and grown through sales. That means that somewhere, some place there are boots on the ground promoting products, services, and ideas. Academia may be too stuck on high level theory to realize that all their strategies, human resource development, diversification plans, and sales forecasts, add up to exactly $0.00 without boots on the ground pushing the products. However, I have come to appreciate that without salespeople, business simply would not exist.

Being a salesperson has taken on some very negative connotations, thanks to some poor business practices. Because of these connotations, many of us shy away from the idea of selling. Instead, we choose to believe that we can get ahead solely on the premise of providing the best service and the best product. Sadly, that is simply not enough. Having the best product and the best service is only valuable if people know about it. The good news is that the "old school" ways and thoughts about selling no longer have to define your sales process. All it takes is to get out in the community with a strong message, a desire to provide great value, and a willingness to serve others through the creation of strong relationships and partnerships. At the end of the day, you have to sell but selling does not have to be a dirty word anymore.

No matter what kind of business you are in, sales produce the income. If you want to grow or even just sustain your business, you must recognize that you have to continually find new customers and clients. I often see struggling businesses try to turn things around by offering new products and services or working on systematizing their processes and procedures. These are great things to do but not in emergency mode. When sales are down (meaning lack of customer traffic), offering new products to customers that don't exist will not fix the problems. When sales are down, the only way to bring things back up is to go out and bring in more traffic.

Of course, the best thing you can do is use effective sales processes to create consistent traffic flow so that you don't ever have to operate in emergency mode. The best way to think of sales processes is to realize that every business has three functions: inside sales, outside sales, and sales support. All three of these business functions work together as one unit to help create a healthy and strong business. If you remove one of the functions, the whole process will implode.

OUTSIDE SALES

I start with outside sales because these are the activities that will increase traffic flow. Whether you have a brick and mortar business, a home business, or an e-business, your primary objective is to generate enough traffic flow to pay the bills and make a decent living. Outside sales help you do just that. Good outside sales skills will meet three objectives:

- Promote value

- Build relationships

- Create partnerships

I used to hate the idea of outside sales. The last thing I wanted to do was run around town knocking on doors, visiting unknown businesses, and making cold calls. I just could not see how any of this would really build a strong and viable business with a good reputation. The thing is, I still don't see it! However, I have changed my perspective on what outside sales actually should be. You can't promote value, build relationships, or create partnerships by bothering people. You may pick up some sales, but eventually you will run out of steam, people, or reputation. The last thing you want is to be known as a pushy and invasive huckster.

Effective outside sales actually doesn't involve selling, at least not your product. Your outside sales duties should sell your brand, your expertise, and your value. What I have learned is that outside sales are simply activities that bring people inside. This includes marketing, tradeshows, networking groups, blogs and social media, and professional organization events.

The key is to lead with your value. Become the expert in your industry and give away plenty of value. By attending or even hosting events in which you can show your expertise, people will start coming to you for advice and relationships will be built. Many of these relationships will turn into partnerships as you find ways to promote each other and work together.

The process goes like this: outside sales should promote value that builds relationships that turn into partnerships. The moment you start thinking of outside sales as selling is the moment your business starts going down a dark road. Keep your business bright by being a valuable part of your community. Try offering free classes or webinars, sponsor local events (and show up to them with a booth), or become an active member of your Chamber of Commerce. There are many ways to give away value and sell yourself to the community. Find the most natural one's for you and your business and dive in head first. Lastly, enjoy! If you are having fun, people will see you as sincere and trustworthy.

INSIDE SALES

Here is where you really promote the product hard. Once you get people through the doors or on the phone, grab them by the jugular and don't let go! No...no...no! This is exactly what you don't want to do. Yet, many businesses treat their customers exactly like that. They lure you in with free value and, before you know it, you're stuck in a Venus Fly Trap. If you don't like it, neither do your customers.

Despite our real fear of becoming a Venus Fly Trap organization, inside sales' ultimate objective is to sell your product or service. I have come to realize that my fear of becoming a pushy salesman has actually hindered my business. I sometimes go overboard to avoid "pushing" someone into a sale. However, I have learned that good sales techniques starts by having a product that you actually believe in. Once you have a product that you know will benefit others, your job is simply to educate people about what you offer. The hard part for me is taking the next leap and actually asking for the sale. However, years of experience has taught me that if you don't ask for the sale, you won't get it. Once someone reaches out to you, it is because they want to buy. Your job is to walk them through the process by meeting three objectives:

- Educate

- Service

- Upsell

If you're like me, you get so excited about your business that all you do is educate your prospects about the numerous great things you offer. The secret is that no one cares! Your customers don't want to discuss the 101 different products or services that you have. All that your customers are concerned with is getting their needs met. In other words, don't spend any time presenting different product options. Instead, spend time learning about what is important to your customers then show them how you can help. This is true whether you are in retail with products to offer or in the service industry. What you sell will help meet your customer's needs. All you have to do is figure out what those needs are and use your knowledge to point them in the right direction.

Everyone knows that good business dictates that we must provide good service, but most people don't categorize this as part of the inside sales process. I do because it helps ease the customer into making the purchase decision. People want to feel special and a large part of the sales process is making that want come true. If your customers feel valued and pampered, they will not only come back, but most likely will purchase more during their visit. If you can't make your customers feel special, but your competitors can, who will they choose? This is where you want to go the extra mile. This is also where the upsell comes in. Part of providing a great experience is making sure that your customers get everything that they need. Sure, the upsell brings in more revenue for you, but it also helps your customers find more value in what you offer. The key to successful upsells is to make it natural. If someone is purchasing a bagel at your coffee shop, naturally ask them if they want cream cheese. If someone is purchasing web development, naturally ask them if they want you to host it. Upselling only becomes annoying to customers if you have a whole list of items that you take them through or if you try to offer them something unrelated to their primary purchase. Done correctly, upselling is a great way of providing extra value and service to your customers.

SALES SUPPORT

If selling is the primary objective of any business, then anything that is not directly related to either inside or outside sales should be considered sales support. Everything that you do should either be a function of direct sales or should support the sales process. Your bookkeeping helps insure positive cash flow is produced from sales. New product introductions give you more to sell. Employee training optimizes sales effectiveness. Processes and procedures help sales go smoothly. Keeping your establishment clean provides customers with a comfortable place for you to sell to them. Technology implementation helps you keep your business organized and frees up more time for you to sell. You get the idea. Always keep your eye on the ball. You are in the sales business. If your time and your team's time is not being spent selling or supporting sales, you're not moving your business forward.

COMMON SENSE IN PRACTICE

Describe your gut reaction to the word salesman. Is it positive or negative?

_____
_____
_____
_____
_____

What event(s) in your life is most responsible for the image you have of sales people?

_____
_____
_____
_____
_____

Describe your current sales process.

_____
_____
_____
_____
_____
_____
_____

Brainstorm the different ways that your product brings value to your customers.

_____
_____
_____
_____
_____
_____

Brainstorm the different ways that you can educate your customers or prospects on the value of your product.

_____
_____
_____
_____

Pick three of the items from the above list that you can start implementing right away.

1._____ 2. _____ 3. _____

BUILD IT AND THEY WILL COME:
BUILDING A BETTER PLAN

For years, I have seen small businesses operate with a "build it and they will come" mentality. The thought process is that "if my product or service is good enough, people will find me." The destruction of any business starts with the myth that your business' success will be driven by the quality of what you offer. Don't get me wrong: providing a quality product or service is paramount to your success. People demand high quality goods. Ultimately, you are in business to sell products that people want to purchase. The trouble begins when you start thinking that your product is a silver bullet. Sure, people will buy your product and keep coming back because it is the best, but don't miss the first step: first, you have to get the people to show up, to hear about you, to want to do business with you.

The harsh reality is that no matter how good your product is, people will not simply "find" you. If you talk to any business person, they will quickly tell you that success is not based on luck, but hard work. Yet, when we operate our own business, we quickly forget to follow our own instruction. We all fall into the trap of thinking that what we have is different, better, or more powerful. We don't say it out loud, but we all think that the rules won't apply to us as we etch "a little luck" into our business plan.

I am sure that your concept is absolutely special and unique, after all you have put your heart and soul into it, and possibility everything else you own. So, doesn't something that wonderful deserve the royal treatment? Instead of believe that your products quality will drive people to find you. Treat your business, your product with the respect and care it deserves. Take out all the stops, and do whatever it takes to make it successful.

WHY CUSTOMERS WON'T FIND YOU

People won't find you because they're not looking. It does not matter what your product or service is, how great it is, or even how much people need it, they're not looking for you. There are a lot of reasons why people aren't looking, but I have found that most of the reasons fall into three broad categories: they already have a provider, they don't know they need what you offer, and they're too busy to notice you.

Business is about putting all the pieces of the puzzle together. Only the full and completed picture allows for success. When we try to pick up just one or two elements of business and say "this is how I will succeed," we inevitably fail. People don't understand what we are offering because we only showed them a few pieces of the puzzle. In order be noticed by customers, we have to be aware of and guard against the three reasons why our customers don't even know we exist.

They Already Have a Provider

Just because you are in a high-demand industry does not automatically make you in high demand, even if you are the best, cheapest, or brightest. Industries like insurance, real estate, auto body, health supplements, restaurants, and coffee shops all make billions of dollars per year, but you still have to work and market yourself to carve out your share. You can name just about any industry and chances are there is a huge market for it. Most likely, that is what attracted you to your industry. You saw others succeeding and believe that you can offer something even better. The questions that you now have to ask yourself are: how will you get noticed, how will you differentiate yourself, and how will you attract enough of the market to become successful? The answers to these questions will help you create the success that you need. Just stay alert and don't fall into the trap of thinking that just because you are a coffee shop, people will stop going across the street and start coming to you.

They Don't Know They Need or Want What You Offer

Just because you open up a unique concept does not mean people will automatically check it out. Your idea may truly be the best thing since sliced bread, but novelty or even quality alone is not enough to insure success. People are creatures of habit and if you want to interrupt their retinue, or become part of their repertoire, you are going to have to get in their face with the right message, targeted to the right people. We talk about this in a lot more detail in the chapter If a tree falls in a deserted forest, does it make a sound.

They're Too Busy to Notice You

I have found this last one to be particularly dangerous for my own businesses. Whether, we are talking about my family's smoothie chain or my books and blogs, I tend to believe that what I offer is unique enough to be noticed by everyone who passes by. If I can just get enough people to walk by, surely success will follow. One example is with my family's smoothie chain. We have always sold espresso. The drinks were on the same menu board as the smoothies. Right below the board was a huge espresso machine, yet people never ordered espresso from us. After realizing that for some reason people were not reading the bottom of the menu boards, or noticing the huge machine right at their eye level on the back counter, we changed things up a bit and created a series of 6 different boards with pictures. 90% of the customers who came in after the change were very excited to learn that we had started serving espresso. People are busy, and if you don't create an impactful message, they simply will not notice you. We knew that our espresso was the best on the block, but it did not matter. We failed to capture people's attention in the right way.

CHEAP LOSERS

Most businesses that I talk to who take the build-it-and-they-will-come approach do so out of fear of spending money. If you are not willing to spend money and invest in the growth of your business, then all you are really left with is the hope that if you build it, they will come. We talk about this in great detail in the chapter, I Robbed Myself, but I will say it here, too: trying to run your business as cheaply as possible will destroy you. The key about business expenses is not to find the cheapest route but to find the most profitable route. It is so easy to look at two options (whether it be for marketing, new products, additional employees, etc.) and quickly pick the least expensive route. The thing is that the least expensive option can actually cost you more. For example, let's say we are looking at two fairly inexpensive coupon marketing options. One option costs $1 per coupon and the other $2.50. Naturally, we will gravitate toward the cheaper option (why not save 1.50?). Now, what if I told you the option for $1 will gross only 25 cents in additional revenue, but the option for $2.50 will bring in $3? By quickly choosing the less expensive option, you lose 75 cents every time someone purchases your coupon deal, but in the more expensive option, you make 50 cents.

The most desperate business people I encounter are the ones that can't figure out why, after being so careful not to spend money, they still end up broke. In this example, the least expensive option is actually the one that at first glance appeared to be way overpriced. As business owners, we face options like this every day. I have had to train myself to always ask which option will bring in more revenue. More times than not, it is the option with the higher investment that will keep our business moving forward and profitable. We need to change the way that we ask questions about business. Instead of asking how much something costs, ask how much income will it generate. Below are three things that you can do to take your success out of the hands of chance, but be aware that they all cost time and money.

REMOVE LUCK FROM YOUR PLAN

1.   We all know that location matters, but does it really? Yes. There is no way around the fact that if you want to maximize your success, you have to pick the better (more expensive) location. Remember: people don't find you because they are too busy, they don't know they need you, or they think they already have someone like you. Blow your competition out of the water by going were the people are. So many businesses think they have to save money on rent, but if there is one place to splurge, this is the place. Your business is 100% based on the amount of people that walk through your doors, log on to your website, or call you on the phone. Don't save a few bucks and wait for people to find you. Spend the extra cash to go to the people. If you are an online store or service provider make sure you spend the extra money to move your business to the top of the search engines. If you're in the service industries, location still matters just as much as if you were a retail shop. People do business with those they recognize and if you are tucked away in some corner waiting for customers to find you, you had better like solitaire.

2.   Advertising is not optional. No, seriously, it is not optional. There are no exceptions. Location matters but, just like my customers who never noticed our giant shiny espresso machine, visibility is not the only factor. Small businesses don't like to spend money on advertising because they don't think it works, but this book has two full chapters devoted to small business advertising tactics that do work. The key to advertising is to start early, keep it consistent, and communicate to the right people. I am a firm believer that your target market are the people that already come to your store. Get their email addresses, have contests to attract repeat business, and/or start a loyalty program. The great thing about advertising is that it is something you can do very cost effectively. There are plenty of ways to reach your customers and grow your base for free, but that does not mean you can neglect paid advertisements. Coupon mailers, Google ad words, and talk radio are all great ways to target your customers. The reason that advertising most often fails for small business is because they get people in the store but don't have measures in place (such as the ones above) to keep them coming back. Advertising is a two pronged attack. First, get them to show up, then get them to keep coming back.

3.   Networking, relationship building, and free value-added services are all ways for you to get connected to your community and your customers. As a business owner you have to be out in the public meeting new people. If you know that you aren't comfortable with that, have a staff

member do it, but if your business is not networking, it is not growing. Schedule 1-2 hours per week to physically go out and grow your business. People are most loyal to those they know. Becoming everyone's friend is a great way to help your business succeed. The mistake that most business owners make (especially service providers) is that they network when they are slow, then drop-off the face of the earth when things get busy. Of course, a few weeks later, things are slow and they're showing back up again. Stay consistent so that your sales stay consistent. You are never too busy to take yourself off the books for an hour a week to grow your company. The only other option is to settle into a roller-coaster ride of up and down sales.

COMMON SENSE IN PRACTICE

In what ways does luck get etched into your business plan?

_____
_____
_____
_____
_____
_____
_____

What can you do to take control of the areas you currently leave to luck?

_____
_____
_____
_____
_____
_____
_____
_____
_____

Which of the three reasons, (1. customers already have a provider, 2. customers don't know they need or want what you offer, or 3. customers are too busy to notice you) most affects your business? Explain.

_____
_____
_____
_____
_____
_____
_____
_____

Brainstorm all the different ways that you can help overcome the three reasons that customer won't find you.

_____
_____
_____
_____
_____

Pick three of the items from the above list that you can start implementing right away.

1._____   2. _____   3. _____

DON'T LET YOUR BUSINESS TAKE YOU FOR A WALK: HOW TO MAINTAIN CONTROL

Ever watched a dog take their owners for a walk? It can really be an entertaining experience to watch. The dog is outstretched, nose down, pulling hard at the leash while the leash holder stumbles along with a look in their eyes somewhere between fear, anger, and embarrassment. It is easy as an onlooker to judge the leash holder. Clearly they hold all the power, yet their authority seems to be running away, as frustration turns into surrender. The dog can only go so far before its leash stops the advance, but the dog has learned not to worry about the leash. He knows all that he has to worry about is controlling the leash holder. The dog has learned that the leash holder does not start the walk with a firm stance, rooted on solid ground, and thus, can easily be pulled wherever the dog wants to go. Most dog trainers will agree that the first step in training a dog is to first train yourself. Dogs respond to confidence and certainty, but if you're not confident in your ability to lead your dog, the dog's pack instincts will insist that HE must become the leader.

The very same thing can happen to your business if you don't understand your own strengths and weaknesses. Most businesses that end up taking their owners for a walk start out with an owner that does not want to take full responsibility for their business. They are always looking for someone to blame or for some grand excuse when things aren't going right. Eventually, their inability to manage themselves erodes the brakes and they find themselves with a runaway business. At this point, it is time to pose the hard question: do you manage your business or does your business manage you? A lot of small business owners actually struggle with the difference between the two. Here are some telltale signs that your business is managing you.

- You wake up stressed every morning thinking about the business

- Nothing gets done if you are not around

- Even though you say you trust your staff, you're always looking over their shoulders

- If you had to, or wanted to leave for a few days, you don't know who to leave in charge

- You're the only one responsible for sales (bringing in new customers or clients)

- You're the only one who understands how the business works as a whole

- You don't trust that your staff will ever meet your expectations

- You're indecisive and often change game plans

- You don't have written policies, procedures, or job descriptions

- You don't have a defined and duplicable sales process

- You don't have a measurable way of reviewing your staff's productivity and effectiveness

- Employee turnover is high

- Customers/clients always expect more out of you than you can actually give

It is really hard to be honest enough with yourself to actually admit to any of the above issues, but let me encourage you to be brave. A business that manages you will eventually overtake you and destroy everything in its path, including itself. You owe it to yourself to take a hard look at the above list and find ways to improve your relationship with your business. If you are not willing to admit your areas of weakness, they will continue to put a wedge between you and your dreams.

When I look at businesses around me that seem to be managing their owners, there are a couple of prevalent issues that magnify the problem. One of the most common is a manger's unwillingness to actually manage their people. They don't take the time to properly train, empower, and coach their employees. This leads to thinking that their employees are never good enough. However, more times than not, it is actually a matter of not properly managing employees' skills, expectations, or performance. The other common issue that I see are customers setting the expectations. You, as the business owner, need to set the expectations. Many business owners believe that allowing the customer to set the expectations is actually a good thing. They believe it demonstrates great customer service. The problem is that a customer's expectation is to get the most out of you for the least amount of money. This often leads to situations in which the customer never feels that their expectations were met. Of course, both these issues can be corrected by simply changing your own thoughts and expectations about how you should run your business.

MANAGE YOUR BUSINESS

If you really want to be the manager of your business, you need to run it with purpose. You have to be in control, but often times that means empowering others. A person who manages their business understands that managing does not mean holding the fort together. It means leading your organization to thrive. You have to set a powerful vision and solid standard and hold your team accountable to your expectations and your plan. Most managers forget the accountability part of their duties. A good manager will spend the bulk of their time motiving their team toward a higher standard through encouragement, training, and correction. The alternative is a business with a frustrated manager who feels that they have to do everything, because they don't trust their employees to get things done right. A manager (or you as the owner) can't be bogged down by doing your employees' work and still expect to maintain control.

If your business is managing you, you will miss opportunities to grow and you will miss the best part of business ownership. Remember the core reason why you started your own business. You wanted flexibility; you wanted to create your own destiny. Well, somewhere along the road your business became the boss. It is time that you take back the captain's chair. What you must remember is the most effective businesses will run without your hands on everything. Take the time to surround your business with process and structure. If you don't mold your business, it will mold you.

SETTING PROPER EXPECTATIONS

I hear it from people all the time. You can hear the frustration and the sadness in their voice. Business owners constantly complain that they bend over backwards for their clients, yet it is never good enough. Why? Is it the business owners fault? Or do clients just have unrealistic expectations?

The real issue is that business owners set themselves up for failure by giving the client unrealistic expectations during the sales process. In my opinion, most businesses misunderstand the sales process. They are so focused on the sale that they fail to realize that this process will set the foundation and the expectation for the whole relationship. There are many different ways that businesses can set themselves up for failure during the sales process. However, they all come down to one thing: they fail to set proper expectations and to take control as the leader of the relationship. It is important that we keep in mind that no one can work very well while bending over backwards. That means if you are having to bend over backwards, you will not be able to produce your best work.

Perhaps the biggest secret in business is that you will never be able to live up to your clients expectations if you let them set the expectations. Use the sales process to tell the client what they should expect. This may seem counterintuitive. We have been taught to believe that providing great customer service is providing the client whatever they want. The problem is that this is not realistic. Ultimately, customers want the world for free and if you don't set clear expectations, they won't be happy until they get the world (for free).

Many frustrated business owners feel like their clients don't respect the fact that the moon was pulled down and handed to them. What we don't realize is that without setting clear expectations, the customer is expecting the whole universe. The funny thing is that clients and customers really will be happy with much less than the moon as long as we are honest and upfront about what we can and will provide. For example, don't just tell clients that you will build them the best widget ever. If you stay that vague, they will expect a robot that transforms into a spaceship and runs on oxygen. Being vague lets your customers imagine whatever they want. That imaginative (and impossible) image of excellence will become their reality. However, if you set the expectation upfront that you will provide the best widget ever built that does a, b, and c, and then go out and create an awesome a, b, and c widget, your client will get exactly what they expected and will be thrilled.

The best way to insure happy clients and customers is not to sell them whatever makes them happy. Instead, tell them that what you provide is exactly what they are looking for. Some of the most successful companies in the world have people happily line up for mediocre products. How? They tell customers exactly what to expect and then make that expectation sound like the greatest thing in the world. No one goes to a fast-food restaurant expecting a fine dining experience, yet most customers walk away happy because they got exactly what they expected. Yet, you go to a fine dining restaurant and their percentage of unhappy customers skyrockets.

The difference is that the fine dining establishment promised the best quality available, but left quality up to interpretation. The fast-food restaurant simply promises fast food, and they hit the mark almost every time. We can't expect our customers to be happy if we don't tell them what happy is.

RUN (DON'T WALK) YOUR BUSINESS

We often overthink the complexity of our business. Don't get me wrong; I don't want to downplay your hard work, but I have learned that simplicity will always create greater success than complexity. If you find yourself overwhelmed and exhausted, it's not fun anymore. If you're not having fun, your business will just become a job. The trick is to keep your business fun. The most successful business owners are the ones that want to go to work every day. This feeling of satisfaction and accomplishment is only possible if you are properly managing your business. In the simplest form, proper management comes down to managing expectations. You must manage your expectations, your employees' expectations, and your customers' expectations. Just like walking a dog, this starts by realizing that you are in control and that you set the pace. People will follow your lead, but if you are not leading, everyone will start pulling on your leash. Take control by pulling in the slack then turn in the direction you want to go and your business will follow.

COMMON SENSE IN PRACTICE

What are your expectations for yourself in your business?

_____
_____
_____
_____
_____
_____
_____
_____
_____

What expectations do you have for your employees?

_____
_____
_____
_____
_____
_____
_____
_____
_____
_____

What should your customers expect?

_____
_____
_____
_____
_____
_____
_____
_____

1. Define products or services

_____
_____
_____
_____
_____

2. Define your customer service values

_____
_____
_____
_____
_____
_____

SHARE THESE EXPECTATION WITH YOUR EMPLOYEES AND CUSTOMERS. THIS EXERCISE IS POINTLESS IF YOU KEEP THE INFORMATION TO YOURSELF.

HONEY I SHRUNK THE BUSINESS:
STAYING BIG IN A SMALL WORLD

We all want our businesses to grow. But how big is too big? Is your dream to create a multinational organization, or do you just want to make a big impact in your community? In today's world, it is hard to stay big. People have less money to spend and more places to spend it. With the advent of mega, online retailers like Amazon and EBay, it can sometimes feel like the only way we will find success is by going huge. I know I have often felt that if I can't become a top player, I should just get out of the game.

Recently, I have realized that that is the point. The large companies want to push me away. They want to make my business look hopeless. No, not because they're heartless. In all fairness, all is fair in love and war. Large corporations are designed to crush their competition, it is really not personal. If you don't want to play, get out of the game...or change the rules. That's when I realized that I was looking at everything all wrong. As a little guy trying to go head-to-head with the giants, I would lose. I realized all I had to do to win was adapt a little PR trick. If you don't like the conversation, change it.

You see, I learned that as a small business, I don't have to compete on the same playing field. In baseball the minor league teams never go up against the major league teams. So why should I? The problem was that I was still thinking like an academic. Academia refuses to acknowledge small business. They only teach and study concepts relevant to the big, publicly-owned companies. To academia, numbers and resources are so large and vast that you just get used to thinking in terms of millions, not thousands, and certainly not hundreds. My annual budget was equal to a large corporation's hourly expenses. Yet, I set out trying to create very miniature versions of the same thing.

Eventually, I realized that academia had it all wrong. They were only looking at about 0.03% of the whole story. According to www.SBA.gov, small business represent 99.7% of all employer firms and are responsible for over 65% of net new jobs over the past 17 years. Small businesses are also responsible for over 95% of all US exports. These ignored (by academia) facts changed the whole story for me. Small business is not the exception to the rule. Small business, as a whole, is the power house. That's why large corporations want us gone: we are actually their worst nightmare (not the other way around), a bunch of individual, non-connected organizations, all utilizing different strategies and tactics. We are impossible to predict and have the international "too big to fail" mega companies surrounded.

MAKE YOURSELF MATTER

Once you realize that you don't have to play the same games as the large, mega companies in order to be successful, you can set the ground rules for your own success. The first rule is to set your own standards. Decide for yourself what makes your organization great. The big common sense key here is that people are attracted to sincerity. When you set standards, expectations, and goals that you are passionate about, people will be attracted to what you have to offer. Of course, the tricky part is that you have to actually judge yourself by the standards that you set. Check your progress and consistency often.

The second rule is to think local but act global. This means that first and foremost your commitment and dedication needs to be to provide local value. Those closest to you should be your biggest fans. No matter where your big dreams take you, every business started by first mastering and conquering their local market. The internet takes some of this need away, but even if you are a 100% ecommerce organization, connecting with your local community will only help ground you to a secure foundation of support, partnerships, and cause.

The "act global" part comes into play by the fact that today's world is getting smaller. The internet connects everyone and opens doors to possibilities once reserved only for the mega organizations. Today, local can be so much more than just geographical region. Close knit communities are all over the internet, based on niche markets of people with similar passions, hobbies, religions, political bents, and professions. A large part of your local community does not have to be in your backyard, but your values and commitment to the community should always stay the same.

The final rule is to stay true to yourself and your original mission. Your business will change and adapt with the times, but always remember your core. The moment you lose sight of why you started your business is the moment it all starts getting away from you. You will increase your product or service mix, change your marketing strategies, add more staff, and maybe even multiple locations, but whatever you do needs to relate back to the original standards, expectations, and goals that you set for your company.

CAPITALIZE ON PEOPLE

Today's global economy has taken people out of the strategy mix. The large international organizations see people as numbers, not as individuals to care for and serve. The internet connects us with pictures and screen names instead of faces and relationships. The bottom line is that it is too easy to forget that you are in business because of each individual customer. Don't take this for granted. The real advantage that small business has over large corporations is that the small business has to care. We can't just look at numbers and make faceless decisions. Our business is in place because we understand our customers' needs and wants. This is something that academia and their large corporations don't understand and it is to our advantage. It is the secret that will help us continue to win market share. People choose us because we know them, and their families, and their dogs, and their passions. Often times, their passions are our passions. These connections are what will always give small business the advantage and the ability to grow.

COMMON SENSE IN PRACTICE

What is most important to your customers?

_____
_____
_____
_____
_____
_____
_____
_____
_____
_____

What values and standards set you as an individual apart?

_____
_____
_____
_____
_____
_____
_____
_____
_____
_____

Do you bring the above values and standards into your business? How can you get better at this?

_____
_____
_____
_____
_____
_____

Brainstorm different ways that you can grow your business by focusing on your values and standards.

_____

_____

_____

_____

_____

_____

Pick three of the items from the above list that you can start implementing right away.

1._____ 2. _____ 3. _____

I ROBBED MYSELF: HOW TO

EFFECTIVELY FIX CASH FLOW ISSUES

Warning! Due to the technical and graphic nature of the content in this section, extreme boredom may overcome you. Reader discretion is advised. Unfortunately, as business owners we cannot overt our eyes. We must understand how cash flow works and how to utilize it to grow our business. But, we will try and make it as fun as possible!

If you have ever taken a college level accounting class, you would have been presented with complex equations, theories, and countless guidelines on industry practices and standards. If you are like me, all you could do during class was go to your happy place and pray for it to be over soon. There were only two things that I got out of my accounting classes: 1) I now really respect accountants and2) at all costs, I wish to avoid that pain again. The problem is that I own a business; I have to at least understand my own books. Over the years, I have realized that small business accounting is not the monster that college made it out to be. I don't have to worry about public records, stock dividends, multimillion dollar debts (hopefully), or currency trading. All I need to worry about is what I bring in and what goes out.

DISCLAIMER

I would be doing you a disservice if I claimed that what I am about to share is the whole story. I have found that the most successful businesses have or outsource an accountant or certified book keeper. I strongly recommend this. For one, they are the experts and can help you with your taxes in addition to keeping your books in order. A good bookkeeper will more than pay for themselves by finding tax credits and by optimizing your cash flow and budget sheets.

Finding the right bookkeeper will free up your time so that you can focus on growing your business. They can also give you valuable advice. Basically, what I am saying is that if you own a business, get a bookkeeper. No exception, no excuses (well, there is one exception...if your business is bookkeeping, than you hopefully have this stuff down).

BILLS: THE NECESSITY OF LIFE

Let's just face the truth: bills scare us to death. They can destroy our motivation and halt us dead in our tracks. I suppose I could give the age-old adage that bill paying anxiety can be eliminated with a good budget. But, that is too predictable, and frankly, not true. Yes, budgeting is a necessity; however, we need to dive deeper than just surface budgeting tricks. Budgeting will help make the fear more predictable, but it does not eliminate it. It simply tells you what days of the month you should be afraid of.

As a business development consultant, I have seen passionate, strong, and confident adults buckle the moment their new business' first bills arrive. I see it all the time. Their training, their planning, their excitement, all out the window as they curl up in the fetal position. Their eyes wide, their bodies trembling, "I can't pay this bill," they protest. The funny thing is that a business without bills is like a ship stranded in the middle of the ocean with no sails. It does not matter how hard the wind blows, you aren't going anywhere. Despite this, so many business owners' first reaction to a bill is to figure out how to avoid getting another one. They end up stranding themselves in deep waters before they ever had a chance.

Before you get too excited, I am not suggesting that the more bills you have the faster you will get to your goals. Just like a ship's sails, bills have to be used with a purpose. What I am suggesting is that avoiding bills, or trying to eliminate, them is never a good plan. Before you can create a sound budget and start looking for ways to effectively cut costs, you have to understand the nature of what a bill is.

A bill is not a bad thing. Say it with me, "A bill is not a bad thing". Bills pay for the products that we sell at a profit, they pay for our employees that produce our services, and they pay for the energy and rent that allow us to operate our business. Bills are tools to help us make money. If you are not making money, it is not the bill's fault. It is the way that the bills are being used to move your company forward.

DON'T ROB YOURSELF

Many business owners see cash flow as a simple matter of keeping expenses low. Unfortunately, it is not that easy. Sure, you want to optimize your expenses and eliminate wasteful spending. However, simply trying to keep your expenses low will cause you to eventually run out of gas. A better question to ask is what needs to be done to increase revenue? The answer will most likely include having to spend some money. Thus, if your mindset is always to spend as little as possible, you will miss opportunities to increase your revenue. If your sales are not increasing, they are declining. There is no such thing as a flat line business, except for a dead one.

The trick to successful spending and cash flow management is to track the results of your spending. Keep good records of everything that you spend and put it up to what I call the profit test: Ask yourself, "did this bill do one or more of the following"?

- Did it help maintain my business (keep the doors open)?

- Did it increase my sales?

That's it: if a bill did not provide one of those two things, spend your money elsewhere. One the other side, if the bill did accomplish one of the two things, keep it! If you try and eliminate it, your business will start to tumble. Think of the bills that maintain your business and increase your sales as if they are the foundation to your company. If you remove even one, the foundation will become unstable. In essence, if your mind set is simply to spend as little as possible, you are robbing yourself. You are taking money that should go back into the business and stealing your own future in the process.

I am being harsh, true, but the bottom line is that a successful business has never been built by cutting needed resources. Yet, this seems to be the most common approach when trying to start up or turn a business around. I know that many companies need to find ways to streamline their organizations, and this can include making tough decisions such as layoffs, plant closures, and operational budget cuts. The difference is that these cuts aren't knee- jerk reactions; they are calculated plans. It's ok to circle the wagons, but with purpose. How do you know what to cut and when to cut it? It all comes back to understanding that bills don't cause failure. The improper use of bills causes the failure.

The improper use of bills comes in two forms:

1. Purchasing things that you don't need.
2. Not purchasing things that you do need.

Most would assume that the second issue is a result of the first, but this is not always true. Many businesses are so afraid to spend money that they end up "saving" themselves out of business. Failing to make proper repairs on equipment and buildings, not hiring the more qualified (and more expensive) employees, reducing inventory levels, substituting lower quality ingredients (or materials)...All of these things are sure fire signs that you are "saving" your business into the ground. This is just as dangerous, perhaps even more so than, spending money on unneeded things. If you start overspending, you can always adjust, but once your company gets a bad reputation because you tried to cut costs in all the wrong places, it is very hard to turn things around.

ACTION PLAN

The best way to keep your business strong is to feed it with needed nutrients. But like any nutritional expert, you have to first understand what your business needs. You accomplish this by planning, implementing, and tracking results. Know your business' numbers and know what makes it tick. It is not enough to throw money at your business. You have to figure out what works through trial and error and as you find solutions that move your company forward, keep them in place. How do you do all this planning and tracking? This is where a strong budget comes in. Think of it as your business' meal plan for a fit and healthy lifestyle. If you don't plan how to spend your money, it will get wasted, overlooked, and misused. Money is simply too easy to spend (and to easy not to spend). A budget helps you prepare and implement a healthy spending plan.

The purpose of a strong budget is to use it as a check and balance for your actual spending. It is best to have a monthly and an annual budget (Hint: the annual budget should equal the sum of the 12 monthly budgets). The monthly budget will help you compare your actual spending to your budgeted spending every month. This is vitally important. A budget does you no good if you don't actually use it as a tool to help you track spending. Revenue from months that you are under budget should be put into an expense savings account for slower months or for months when you happen to go over budget.

Most of what we have talked about is common sense, but I believe that it is important to stick with the basics. Business does not have to be complicated and simplicity is often the most effective tool. The key take-aways from this lesson is that you need to create a strong habit of checking your budget to actual expenses, don't be afraid to spend money where and when it is needed, and to think of bills as the food that keeps your business going. Don't rob your future by starving your business.

COMMON SENSE IN PRACTICE

Write down monthly expenses that sustain your business.

_____

_____

_____

_____

_____

_____

_____

Write down monthly expenses that help your business grow.

_____

_____

_____

_____

_____

_____

_____

Write down expenses that don't sustain or grow your business. Why do you have them?

_____

_____

_____

_____

_____

_____

List some expenses that you avoid, but would help your business grow if you made the investment. Why are you afraid to spend money on your company's future?

_____

_____

_____

_____

_____

_____

_____

_____

_____

WHAT WILL TOMORROW BRING? HOW TO CREATE A PLAN FOR THE FUTURE

I have had to learn the hard way that the future is unpredictable. I started out my career arrogantly, thinking that my path was set, that I was on my way to all my dreams coming true. I suppose that this is the fate of most young people. They tend to think they are bulletproof. I am honestly not sure we ever grow out of this mentality. We just get more sophisticated with how we approach the future. We look for the perfect plan, the perfect opportunity, or the perfect chance to lock in our dreams. Of course, all the while we are asking ourselves, "What will tomorrow bring?" How does one plan for the unknown? How do we lasso in the future in order to take control of our destiny?

"Carpe Diem," is perhaps a phrase you have heard way too often. However, it is a good phrase. Carpe Diem (Seize the Day) is something that business professionals all need to get better at. As students, most of us heard this phrase at our graduation ceremonies. Students are encouraged to look to their future and seize the day along the way. It seems that as we get older and more focused on our life's plans, we forget the Carpe Diem part. We get so busy planning and conspiring for our future that we forget to take advantage of the moment. This is not just an inspirational, feel-good idea: Carpe Diem has very practical implications. How often do we lose on opportunity in front of us because we are planning for future opportunities?

Planning is important but sometimes we get so stuck in planning mode that we never really get anywhere. All we do is plan and then plan some more. At some point, a plan has to be implemented. Our plans should be used to help propel us forward, but more times than not, they keep us stuck. This is not the plan's fault. It is the way that we think of planning that causes these issues. When we are in planning mode, all we can see and think of is what's beyond the horizon. For those of us who always live in planning mode, this means that daily tasks, duties, and opportunities are often missed.

We only notice the things that we deem important, and we only care about what we notice. These words may be harsh, but they have serious implications in our business, personal, and social lives. In today's fast-paced world there is so much that we miss, so much that we don't notice. The idea behind the statement is not so much that people don't care, but that we are just really bad observers. Perhaps it is too easy to not notice. We are all bombarded with radio ads in which we can change the station, TV commercials that we can fast forward, billboards that we can look the other way from, and internet ads that simply pop up and disappear in the corner of our eyes. Our modern world has taught us how to filter out everything except that which we deem important at the moment.

What does that mean for all the things happening around us that we should notice and should care about, but don't? As business professionals it is way too easy to prioritize our day then hunker down and check items off of our list. But is that really living and is that really productive? Sure, things get done but what did we miss along the way? It is time that we learn to un-filter our lives. Yes, at first glance this sounds a little scary and could be distracting, but sometimes distractions can be good things.

In our unfiltered vision, we can see our business, our lives, and even the world as a whole. Think about the amazing opportunities that could bring; opportunities to help and serve, but also opportunities to prosper. Unfiltered vision could give us cause to stop at the corner to give a dollar to the homeless, we could notice when our spouse needs a second hug goodbye, and we could notice better ways to operate our businesses. Unfiltered vision brings a clearer picture about what is important, where the needs truly are, and how to interact effectively with our surroundings.

Right now, we're all walking around with filtered vision, stumbling along until we run into something meaningful and worthwhile. Let's take off our goggles and learn to observe, notice, and care. I think we would all be surprised just how far a few worthwhile distractions can take us.

The key is to plan for the future, but seize the day along the way. We must learn that there is no time like the present to seek out new opportunities, to enjoy the life and the day that we are in, and to make a difference in our business and in those lives that surround us. Plan to prepare, but don't wait to start your life until you get to step Z.

So how do you create a plan for tomorrow? Just in case you missed the hint, you start by living today. In all honesty worrying about the future does not do you any good. We don't know what tomorrow will bring, but I can guarantee you that if you live well and work hard today, tomorrow won't look so scary. Tomorrow's success starts with what you are doing today. The next day is simply a continuation of what you make important, of the standards you set, and of the people you impact.

The best way to live for today is to have a clear focus of where you are now and were you want to be. It is important to spend some time dreaming and planning for tomorrow. It will help guide your daily actions. I have found when I'm planning it is helpful to use a consistent structure to help build an implementable plan. That is the key word, "implementable." When you do plan, you need to create actual action items that you can accomplish daily. Simply saying that you want to grow your business 20% by next year won't actually make it happen. This is where most people go wrong with their planning. They create a list of things that they want, and maybe put together a budget, but without clear-cut nonnegotiable action items, a plan is all hype.

1. Start by dreaming. Write down all the things that you want to accomplish in a given time frame (one year, 6 months, etc.). Think of this as a brainstorming session. Don't edit the ideas.
2. Next narrow down your dreams into actual goals that you can accomplish within your given time frame.
3. Now spend some time going over your current position. Where do you stand in the market? Where do you stand in relation to your future goals?
4. Now start listing action items to help you meet your goals. For example, if you want to increase sales by 20%, figure out how much more you need to sell every day and list the ways that you will go get those extra sales.
5. A plan is like a path. This means that you should literally be able to see yourself moving along the plan towards your goals. Come back to your plan at least once a week and check your progress. Make adjustments as needed.

Remember that a plan is not about keeping your eyes on the future. The plan is there to help you know what you need to do today. Don't get overwhelmed by big plans, just take it one day at a time. Celebrate your successes along the way. Lastly, keep yourself open to new opportunities that present themselves. Plans can be changed. In fact, a good plan is open to adaptation. Now, go create your plan and then start living!

COMMON SENSE IN PRACTICE

Brainstorm all the things that you want to accomplish in a given time frame (one year, 6 months, etc.).

_____
_____
_____
_____
_____
_____
_____

Narrow down and define your dreams into actual goals that you can accomplish within your given time frame.

_____
_____
_____
_____
_____
_____

Spend some time going over your current position. Where do you stand in the market? Where do you stand in relation to your future goals?

_____
_____
_____
_____
_____
_____
_____

List action items to help you meet your goals.

_____

_____

_____

_____

_____

_____

_____

RUNNING ON A TREADMILL ONLY GETS
YOU TIRED AND STINKY

Life is busy. I get it. But do your clients? Let us dispel a myth right now. Being busy does not make you look more important than you really are. How many of us make a show of being busy in front of our clients, vendors, and employees? We take a call in the middle of a conversation, just to tell the person on the other end that we are too busy to talk right now. We leave hurried instructions on a voice mail. We don't take the time to spellcheck our e-mails. Is your rushing really effective? Sure, you got a lot done, but what are the results of your work? I call this running on a treadmill because people that operate in this mentality never get anywhere. They run themselves dizzy but at the end of the day, they're tired and stinky. No one wants to be around them, and they are essentially right where they started.

For those of us who love to rush, the point is to realize that every day we are engaging in relationships. So, slow down, look people in the eyes, and engage in the moment. Don't move until the moment is over and then focus your attention on the next task or person in front of you. Show respect to others by being willing to devote your full attention to them for the few moments that it requires. This truly is the only way to step off the treadmill and actually start moving forward. The odd thing is that once you step off, you will feel like you've slowed down and be tempted to hop right back on. What we must realize is that even though we slowed down in speed, we are now getting somewhere. Being busy for the sake of being busy is never effective. Moving a company forward means taking the time to fully engage and devote yourself to each task at hand. Trying to get too many things done may seem efficient but it is never effective.

If you want to truly be effective, you must be engaged in the moment that you are in. Show those around you that you respect their time by turning off your phone until after your conversation. Let those that call leave a message and then get back to them only when you have time to dedicate to their call. People will respect you more for fully engaging with them. When you are talking with staff and vendors, take the time to communicate with them. Slow down and don't think that you can leave valid instructions at 100 miles per hour. You will find that by slowing down your life, you will become less stressed, you will be more productive, your relationships will blossom, and ultimately you will gain long- term success and respect from others.

One of the reasons that we inadvertently end up on the treadmill is because we simply book too many things in a day, then stress trying to get everything done. If you want to get off the treadmill you have to learn how to properly manage your time by putting constraints on your day, and realizing that some things are best left for tomorrow.

TIME MANAGEMENT

Are you at war with time? Many business owners and executives find themselves shocked at the end of every work day because the day is over and their lists of high priority items is still incomplete. The excuses we give ourselves are always the same: "My time is just too unpredictable", "I ran out of time", or "there is not enough time."

The ironic thing about our surprise at the end of the day is that time is very predictable. 8am starts at the same time every day and 6pm comes around exactly on time. This leads me to believe that time has been framed. Instead of realizing that we are not as productive as we should be, we blame time for all our woes.

If we want to be really honest with ourselves, we don't have a time problem. Figuring out a way to have 28 hour days won't solve our issues, and working 12 hour days instead of 8 has not solved the problem either. You see, we don't have a time problem at all. We have a productivity problem and a priority problem. No matter how few or how many hours we give ourselves to work, there is always something in the way of a cleared to-do list.

Now that we are being honest, let's face the fact that no matter how rich and powerful we are (or not), we can't change time. We can't add any, we can't rewind it, and we can't pause it. Everyone lives under these same constraints. I know this seems obvious but we all use time as an excuse. As long as we continue to believe that complaining about time will help our productivity, our issues we will never change.

What we need to do is not blame time, but respect it. Once we can come to terms with the fact that time dictates our days through its natural constraints, we can start to move forward. It is not time that is unruly in our lives. No, we are unruly to the unchangeable facts of time. Now that we have that straight, what can we do about it? How do we gain productivity by respecting time?

The answer to this question will be slightly different for every person, but the main point is that we must realize that there are only so many hours in a day. This means that if we have things that need to get done, we have to prioritize our tasks, then block the time out to complete them. If we continue to walk around, oblivious to the unyielding power of time, it will continue to win the battle. However, if we settle down into a prioritized schedule and sign a peace treaty with time, productivity and a completed check list will follow.

COMMON SENSE IN PRACTICE

Write down some examples from your life or business in which you spent too much time on the treadmill.

_____
_____
_____
_____
_____
_____

Write down a couple of examples about how rushing around has hurt your business, reputation, or relationships.

_____
_____
_____
_____
_____

Brainstorm some ideas you can put in place do help you get off the treadmill.

_____
_____
_____
_____
_____

Pick three of the items from the above list that you can start implementing right away.

1._____   2. _____   3. _____

Are you at war with time? Explain.

_____
_____
_____
_____
_____
_____
_____

Brainstorm different ways you can better manage your time and increase productivity in your life.

_____
_____
_____
_____
_____
_____

Pick three of the items from the above list that you can start implementing right away.

1._____ 2. _____ 3. _____

MY MISSION STATEMENT

IS BROKEN

I often wonder if we have complicated ourselves out of common sense. It seems like the more "sophisticated" we get, the less we think about the simple things like trust, fairness, and integrity. With all our fancy theories and complicated solutions about business, at the end of the day, all we are left with is a trust problem. The American consumer does not trust the American business. We have equations, quotas, benchmarks, and internal and external strategies...all to help us interact with people. Yet in so many cases, all of these "tools" have made the American business un-human. We have trained ourselves to believe that success is bread from coercion, and power is born from heartlessness.

I know what you are thinking: small business is different. We stand as beacons of what once was. We prove that a man's word still holds value. But are we really innocent? Our complicated world has put the small business at a disadvantage; we are underdogs in a world we created. America was built on the backs of small business, but we stand forgotten and all but lost in a world too big to fail. This reality has made the small business shrewd and hungry for what was stolen from it. Our actions and motives are not that different from the large corporations that we condemn as mindless drones. We want to grow, thus we often emulate the large organizations, filling our one-man businesses with so much bureaucracy that we can honestly look an unsatisfied customer in the eyes and tell them it is just corporate policy. Businesses large and small have complicated themselves out of touch with the world. The way we treat our employees to the way we handle customers is all a reflection of what we have become.

Ok, enough with the doom and gloom. I think you get my point. We are all guilty on some level of preferring dogma over common sense. We are all guilty on some level of losing focus and forgetting why we started our business in the first place.

CAN A MISSION STATEMENT FIX THE PROBLEM?

I hear a lot of small businesses say that Mission Statements don't matter. They complain that these statements have never helped them in their business ventures and are just a waste of time. In a lot of ways, this is true. Mission statements don't work because we don't take what they say seriously. Going back to the issue at hand, American consumers don't trust American business because businesses don't match what they say with what they do. As a consumer, I make decisions on which companies I will do business with based on what the company says it stands for. I want to partner with organizations that have strong values, but there is nothing more frustrating than locking arms with an organization only to find that its words are stronger than its actions. For example, the moment a company that boasts great customer service fails to provide said services...the whole reputation goes out the window.

The problem is that we put too little value on our own words. Mission statements, along with all the other promises we make to customers, have been distorted into a slogan or a marketing tactic with fine print that says "actual results may vary." We have to learn to take what we say seriously. Our mission statement can't just be some fancy, feel-good words; it needs to be our business doctrine and when we make a promise to our customers, there should never be any fine print. As business owners, we need to strive to bring back integrity and honesty. There is no reason for us to use fine print if we simply say what we mean. Ultimately, it is a small percentage of businesses and professionals that give our industries a bad rap, but if we are not doing everything in our power to insure that our own words are truth, then we are all guilty.

It is easy to point the blame at everyone else and to argue that we are different. We have to strive every day to treat our customers better than our competition. But I believe that there is more to the story than just customer service and product quality. If we want to change the world through our business, or even if we just want to bring back some faith to the American consumer, we have to stand for more than just good customer service and a quality product. Our mission statement needs to be more of an integrity statement. At the surface, any business can put on a front and provide good service and even a great product. What I am talking about is deeper: what is at the heart of your company? Even deeper, what is in your heart as the owner?

COMMON SENSE IN PRACTICE

Write down your mission statement below (if you don't have one now is a great time to write one). A proper mission statement should be concise and to the point (max. five sentences). Narrow your old one down if you have to.

_____
_____
_____
_____
_____
_____

Now break your mission statement up into 3-6 key points. These points will serve as a promise to your customers about how you will treat them and what kind of product you will offer.

1._____   4. _____

2. _____   5. _____

3. _____   6. _____

How can living out these key points change the face of your business?

_____
_____
_____
_____
_____
_____
_____
_____
_____

COMMON SENSE DEVELOPMENT

On a scale of 1-10 how well have you maintained your mission statement? ____

Write down four ways in which you can improve how you live out your mission statement.

1. _____   3. _____

2. _____   4. _____

I HAVE A PLAN...

...NOW WHAT?

It seems like every business expert or consultant you talk with wants to tell you just how important a good business plan is. I don't think I have ever sat through a single sales training or leadership seminar without being told that my business won't succeed without a written business plan. But what exactly is this mystical document? How can a piece of paper actually dictate my success? It can't! However, a proper plan combined with the implementation of that plan will make or break your business. The issue is not the plan but the emphasis that experts put on planning as opposed to implementing. Yes, you need a plan, but a dry overcomplicated piece of paper called the "business plan" holds no power without the ability to implement the plan.

Many business owners start out strong in the planning phases of their business. They lay everything out with exact precision. They read all the books they can on success and business. They purchase their business cards then sit down at their desks and wait for the phone to ring. Planning is only effective if it leads to action. That is why I say that you don't need a business plan. You need an action plan. If your plan is just collecting dust then you can be assured that success will not find you, but if your plan is worn and weathered from overuse, you are on the right track.

In my opinion, there are two different kinds of business plans. There is The Bank's version used to get a loan. This document is the classic boring, academic, fairly useless document, that must follow rigid guidelines. If you are looking for funding from a bank or an investor, you're simply going to have to grit your teeth and bear writing the document, or pay someone to write it for you. If you want money loaned, there is no way around this fact. Don't try to cut corners here. If you really need the loan, your business plan will make the difference. The problem is that these plans are so cumbersome that that don't actually lend themselves to implementation. They are such a nightmare to write that once you have completed it and gotten your loan, you never want to see it again. They have their purpose, but after you have your loan, you need a written plan that can actually help you move forward. You need an action plan.

BUILDING AN ACTION PLAN

whether you have written a traditional business plan or not, the most important document that you can put together is your action plan. As it sounds, action plans lay out what you are going to do, how you are going to do it, and when you're going do it. With the traditional business plan, your audience is investors and bankers, but with the action plan, the audience is yourself and your staff. That means that you should write it in the way that best inspires action and meaning for you and your team. I believe that an action plan is never complete. t is a document that is always being updated to meet current needs, hurdles, and situations. An action plan should have four parts, with each section getting more defined as you go.

1.   Define your organization. This section should list what your company does; provice the mission statement, core values, and standards of excellence. This is the section that defines your company culture, your work ethic, and the driving reason why you are in business. Unless your company makes a drastic industry change, this section will stay relatively untouched once finalized.

2.   Set your three-year goals. Use this section to broadly state were you want to be over the next three years. Goals have to be quantifiable. For example, instead of saying that you want to be known as the best in the industry (who defines "best" and how to you know if you really are?), state that you want to increase your revenue or production by 50% within the next three years. Goals must be things that you can control. Saying that you simply want to be the best is out of your control because it is too vague.

3.   Set your one-year plan. Once a year, sit down and write out your yearly goals. These are goals from your three year plan that you want to accomplish within the next 12 months. Most importantly, take the time to review where you are in relation to your three year plan, and define what needs to be accomplished to keep you on track. For example, the one year plan should address the following:

a.   Success and Shortcomings from last year's goals

b.   What needs to happen this year to keep things on track?

c.   This year's actual goals.

4.   Set your three-month objectives. Every three months, take the time to get extremely detailed about what you need to accomplish in order to meet your yearly goals. This is the section where you really lay out what has to be done. Bullet points are fine, but be specific. Create objectives and tasks with firm deadlines to help guide you through your plan. It is important to do this every three months to insure that you are on the right track and to make quick adjustments as needed. In fact, three months is really just the minimum; you may find it helpful to take one hour a month to create monthly objectives and tasks.

USING YOUR ACTION PLAN

The great thing about an action plan is that most of it can be written using bullet points and task check lists. This makes the document relatively easy to write and even easier to review and follow. Remember that the purpose of this document is to give you a guide. The contents of the document should help create your corporate culture and bring everyone onto the same page. The document also helps you check your progress by actually seeing things checked off as you complete them. The action plan can be incorporated into your staff training, into your budget planning, and even into your traditional business plan (if applicable). Best of all, action plans will help you prioritize your day by highlighting what needs to be accomplished. Don't be tempted to pass over this simple advice. Action plans are designed to be to the point and relevant to your actual business. Don't get caught up in stressing over format or rules. Just make sure that your plan defines and organizes your tasks, objectives, and goals in a way that inspires you to move forward and capture your dreams.

COMMON SENSE IN PRACTICE

List all the different ways that having a step by step action plan could help your business grow.

_____
_____
_____
_____
_____
_____
_____
_____
_____
_____
_____
_____

Often times, we start out strong in the planning stages, but then never actually implement the plan. What can you do to prevent this from happening?

_____
_____
_____
_____
_____
_____
_____
_____
_____
_____
_____
_____

The final task is to create your action plan. Use the outline below as a guide to create your plan.

Action Plan Outline

- Define your organization

  o Mission Statement

  o Purpose Statement

  o Values and Ethics

- Set your three-year goals

- Set your one-year plan

  o Success and Shortcomings from last year's goals

  o What needs to happen this year to keep things on track?

  o This year's goals

- Set your three-month objectives

CONCLUSION

As you move on through life and business remember to always listen to Common Sense. Remember that life, business, your relationships, and your success are all closely related to who you are as a person. Business is not complicated, but it is full of challenges, challenges that can only be overcome with a clear head, a good heart, and a sound conscience. Common Sense teaches us more than all the theories and advanced courses on business ever could. A sound understanding of the concepts, skills, and strategies of business is a necessity, but they are only part of the equation. Honed skills without a caring hand are useless. Grand strategies without a people-first mentality just leads to corruption and failure.

Common Sense dictates that as leaders we recognize the amazing position we are in and never take that for granted. The people in our lives (whether they be our customers, employees, or friends and family" look to us, but we also must remember to look to them. Leadersh p is a symbiotic relationship between the leader and the led. This relationship is balanced on the idea of mutual respect, as one cannot survive without the other. As you conclude this workbook and continue to move forward in life, never take for granted the position you are in to pos tively affect those around you. Your business can only be as strong, successful, influential, and integral as you are. If you want to change your business, you need to first change yourself.

ABOUT THE AUTHOR

Mark Zarr has a Master's in Business Administration from Liberty University and a BA in Organizational Communication and Structure from Montana State University.

Mark is the owner and founder of Common Sense Development, which specializes in creating and offering small business leadership development tools and educational resources. In conjunction with Common Sense Development, he also owns Rent Your MBA, a consulting firm designed to construct and implement small business solutions, marketing, growth strategies, small business rescue, and employee development programs. He also serves as an adjunct faculty member in the business department at the College of Western Idaho

Mark has been a leader in developing and training people for over 10 years. He has created sales and leadership training programs for a variety of companies and franchises. His career also includes helping his family's regional franchise expand from one location to 12 locations throughout five states in just over four years.

Mark is available to speak to your organization, church, or business on how redefining the way we think about and run our organizations can change the world by leading with a common sense, people-first mentality. Contact Mark at www.MarkZarr.com.

Please visit Mark's websites below to learn how he can help you grow your team, your leadership, and your business.

www.RentYourMBA.com

www.CommonSenseDevelopment.com

www.MarkZarr.com

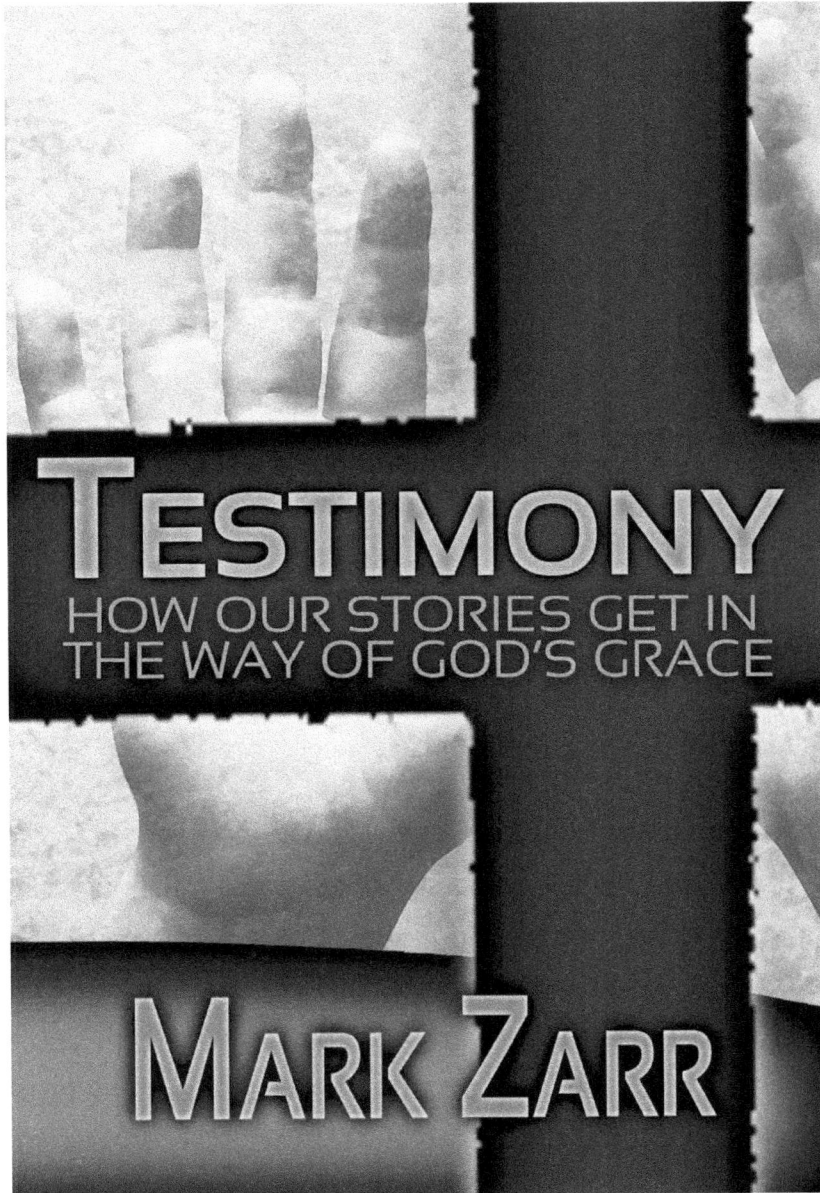

TESTIMONY

HOW OUR STORIES GET IN
THE WAY OF GOD'S GRACE

MARK ZARR

TESTIMONY

HOW OUR STORIES GET IN THE
WAY OF GOD'S GRACE

Have you ever been disappointed by the church? Do you find yourself feeling as if you are on the outside looking in? For many of us church, religion, and even God seem to be unattainable. Whether we have been burned, never truly accepted, or lost in the sea of programs and church growth strategies, we all sense that something is off. Where is the Grace, Love, and Mercy that Christ came to share with us all? Miraculous stories abound of lives that have been turned around. But where is the proof of changed lives?

The truth is that God's grace is for everyone. We have all fallen short, but that is only the beginning of our story. Only God's testimony is powerful enough to save us from ourselves. Our story should not be told in words, but should be lived and explored through our daily walk. We should not merely *talk* about grace, and mercy, and love, when we have been given the amazing gift, by Christ's death and resurrection, to *show* grace, mercy, and love. Our real testimonies are defined not by who we were, but by who we are willing to become.

* 9 7 8 0 6 1 5 6 9 3 4 7 7 *